Willy the Wisher and Other Thinking Stories

Clara Barton School
ECIA Program

Willy the Wisher and Other Thinking Stories

AN OPEN COURT THINKING STORY® BOOK

CARL BEREITER / VALERIE ANDERSON

Language Arts Curriculum Development Center

OPEN COURT  LA SALLE, ILLINOIS

OPEN COURT and ✻ are registered in the U.S. Patent and Trademark Office.

Copyright © 1989, 1983 Open Court Publishing Company

All rights reserved for all countries. No part of this book may be reproduced by any means without the written permission of the publisher.

Printed in the United States of America

ISBN 0-8126-0201-3

Contents

	Introduction	vii
1.	Mr. Sleeby Thinks He's a Giant	2
2.	Willy the Wisher	4
3.	The Thing That Went Under the Door	7
4.	Something Green for Mrs. Nosho	9
5.	Ferdie and the Pot	12
6.	Willy and Mrs. Nosho	15
7.	Poor Old Bowser	18
8.	The Woman with the Wood	20
9.	Would You Rather Have the Dog?	23
10.	The House Where Sleeby Dwells	27
11.	How Mr. Sleeby's House Got That Way	31
12.	The Shovel in the Basement	35
13.	Portia's Birthday	38
14.	Mark Wraps a Present	40
15.	I Forgot What You Needed	43
16.	Mr. Mudanza	46
17.	Manolita Loves Magic	50
18.	Mrs. Nosho in Her Yard	53
19.	It's Hard Work to Be a Boss	56
20.	First Things First	59
21.	Manolita's Real Magic	62
22.	Mrs. Nosho Gets Ready for a Trip	65
23.	Mr. Sleeby Tells About the Circus	68
24.	Mark at the Bath	71
25.	Mr. Mudanza Buys Christmas Presents	74
26.	Manolita's Answer Machine	78
27.	The Chicken Who Practiced to Be Queen	81
28.	Ferdie and the Big Boys	84

29.	Manolita's Second Magic Machine	87
30.	The Farmer Who Found a Giant in His Barn	91
31.	Two of Everything	94
32.	Coffee at Grandmother's House	97
33.	Mr. Sleeby's Toy Store	100
34.	The Three Bowsers	103
35.	Loretta Delivers the Valentines	106
36.	What's Your Trouble, Mr. Sleeby?	110
37.	Willy Keeps On Wishing	113
38.	Mr. Sleeby Buys New Furniture	116
39.	The New Neighbors	119
40.	Mark the Builder	122
41.	Willy's Lost Kitten	125
42.	Mr. Mudanza Changes Things for Mr. Sleeby	128
43.	I Know All About Goldilocks	132
44.	Portia's Lost Shoe	135
45.	Mr. Sleeby Jumps	138
46.	The Lion Who Roared like a Waterfall	141
47.	How to Get Exactly What You Want	144
48.	I Know All About Mr. Sleeby	147
49.	The Pig in the Tree	150
	Index of Stories	153

Introduction

What Is a Thinking Story® ?

A Thinking Story is a kind of "think-along." The stories are real stories, designed to be read by an adult to children, but the children do not merely listen and enjoy. As a story unfolds, the children are asked questions that prompt them to think *ahead* of the characters in the story—to spot what is wrong with what a character has done or said, to anticipate what is going to happen as a result, or to think of other possibilities that the character hasn't considered.

The characters are special. All have highly individualized ways of thinking, and the children learn to recognize them.

Mr. Sleeby is always forgetting things. The children learn to keep in mind the kinds of things that Mr. Sleeby forgets.

Ferdie, impulsive and overconfident, is always leaping to conclusions. The children learn to consider the facts that Ferdie ignores.

Portia, Ferdie's sister, is more cautious. She does not jump to conclusions, and thus often provides a balance to Ferdie's impulsiveness.

Mrs. Nosho is so vague that people have trouble understanding what she is talking about. The children learn how to say things more clearly and to ask the kinds of questions that are needed to find out what Mrs. Nosho means.

Mr. Breezy usually says too much. In trying to be helpful, he confuses people with irrelevant details. The children learn to distinguish the essential from the irrelevant in what Mr. Breezy says.

Mark, Mr. Breezy's son, questions people until he gets complete information; he thus finds things out when others fail. The children learn to anticipate Mark's questions.

Manolita thinks everything happens by magic. The children learn to figure out how things really happen.

Mr. Mudanza, Manolita's father, always changes things "a little." (Given a new dresser, he throws away everything but one drawer and turns that into a wagon.) The children learn to perceive, through mental imagery, the results of Mr. Mudanza's changes.

Willy only wishes for what he wants to happen. The children learn to think of ways to make things really happen.

The troubles that these characters have with thinking are troubles that children themselves often have, but in the stories they are presented in such exaggerated form that the children can hardly overlook them. The characters retain their peculiarities throughout, but later stories present increasingly subtle or complex problems for the children to deal with. The problems never become "brain busters," however, or anything approaching that. From beginning to end, the stories are written to provide light-hearted intellectual fun rather than matter for serious cogitation.

A Few Do's and Don'ts

Since a Thinking Story is different from an ordinary story and also different from a lesson, the adult who reads these stories to children will find the following suggestions valuable:

Read the story the way it's written. Often adults tell stories in their own words instead of reading them as they are written; this is a good idea if the stories are hard or long. But these stories are neither hard nor long, and details that may seem unimportant where they appear become important later. Also, the particular wording is often essential for providing a clue or for not giving a problem away.

Stay on the track. Many of the questions *could* be discussed at length but shouldn't be, because the children would lose the thread of the story. The questions are written for brief answers that move the children on to the next point in the story rather than to related issues. Even if children at first show an inclination to go off on tangential discussions, they will soon come to prefer getting on with the story, as long as the reader doesn't encourage such digressions. Freewheeling discussion is fine, but these stories are not a good vehicle for it.

Use pacing and emphasis to facilitate thinking. Read each story clearly and methodically enough to let the points sink in. Give the children time to think about each question, but not so much time that they forget the point. Make it clear, by voice and by eye contact, whether you are reading narrative or directing a question to the children. The text helps in this by setting off in boldface type the questions to be asked. Emphasize, by a pause and a fresh start, when you are leaving one point and shifting to another one. Otherwise the children may think you are responding to their answers when you are actually going on to a new event.

Think along with the children. Try to maintain an attitude which shows that the important thing is to think carefully about the questions, not to know the answers instantly. Ask the children how they figured out their answers. Allow some debate, since working through arguments can lead to good thinking.

Make the children feel good about their answers. Don't praise children only when they give the answers you happen to have in mind. Recognize that for most questions there are a number of possible answers and that even a clearly incorrect answer probably entailed some worthwhile thinking on the child's part. Try to show a lively interest in the questions and the answers, whatever they may be.

Don't encourage snobbery. The characters in these stories are all well aware of one another's foibles. They are all warm-hearted people who support each other and treat each other with respect. The stories are written so as to convey this attitude to the children as well. A lapse in thinking is not necessarily more contemptible than a broken arm, although both are handicaps that one does well to recognize and avoid if possible. So don't ridicule the characters or make a point of the children's intellectual superiority over them.

Keep a light touch. The stories are often farcical. Many of the questions call attention to something amusing. The stories are not intended to have any drama or serious message, so don't try to invest them with either.

Although this list of strictures may seem a bit imposing, if they are followed at the start it will soon be found that they indicate the most natural way of handling the thinking stories. If the stories are handled successfully, the children will keep asking for more. But they won't say "read another story"; they'll say "do another story." At bottom, that's what thinking stories are—something that adults and children *do* together.

Willy the Wisher and Other Thinking Stories

Mr. Sleeby Thinks He's a Giant

"I don't have a coat," said Mr. Sleeby. "I guess I'll have to go downtown and buy one." So he put on his coat and started out the door.

What is silly about what Mr. Sleeby did? (He said he had no coat but then put one on.)

Then Mr. Sleeby remembered that he didn't have a shirt on, so he went back and put a shirt on over his coat.

Was that the right thing for Mr. Sleeby to do? Why not?

Mr. Sleeby twisted and grunted as he put the shirt on. "This shirt is hard to get on," he said. "Either I'm getting fatter or this shirt is getting smaller."

What's another reason why Mr. Sleeby's shirt was hard to get on?

Then Mr. Sleeby remembered that he hadn't put any socks on. He pulled and pulled the socks on. It took all his strength to get them on. "Dear me," he said, "these socks are too small, too. Perhaps I'm turning into a giant."

What's a good reason why Mr. Sleeby's socks were too small? (He had his shoes on.)

Mr. Sleeby Thinks He's a Giant 3

Willy the Wisher

Willy was always wishing. He hardly ever did anything else. He started wishing when he got up in the morning and kept on wishing all day.

Every morning before school Willy went up to his room to play. Every morning he tripped over his toy truck, which was in the doorway.

"I wish I didn't keep tripping over that truck all the time," he thought.

Will wishing make Willy stop tripping over that truck?
What should Willy do?

Willy never thought to pick up the truck.

Willy carefully stepped over the pieces of train track that were all over the floor, but he accidentally kicked over his toy train.

"I wish the train was running around the track," he thought.

Will the train run around the track if Willy just keeps wishing?
What should Willy do?

Willy never thought to put the track together and put the train on it.

Willy looked up at a big book on the shelf.
"I wish I knew if that book had interesting pictures in it," he thought.

What should Willy do?

Willy never thought to look in the book.

Willy was still standing there, looking up at the book, when he began to feel cold.
"I wish the wind wouldn't keep blowing through that window," thought Willy.

What should Willy do?

Well, Willy didn't do anything to the window. He just stood there wishing, and the wind kept blowing in the window.

Willy got colder and colder. He looked at his sweater, which was in a heap on the floor.

"I wish that sweater was keeping me warm," he thought. "But it isn't."

What should Willy do?

Willy never thought to put on the sweater.

Willy's father called to him from downstairs, "It's time to leave for school, Willy!"

Willy wished he was already at school. He sat down in his chair so he could wish better, but there was a toy airplane in the chair.

"I wish it didn't hurt so much to sit on this toy airplane," he thought. "It has sharp points."

What should Willy do?

Willy never thought to take the airplane off his chair.

Five minutes later Willy was still sitting in the same place, wishing that he was already at school and also wishing that he wasn't so cold and that the airplane didn't hurt so much.

His father came in. "Willy!" he said. "I thought you'd left for school long ago. You'll be late."

Willy's father closed the window, gave him a jacket, and sent him out the door.

Nobody else was in sight. Willy could see the school, but he couldn't see anybody going in and he couldn't see anybody walking to school.

Why couldn't Willy see anybody else walking to school?

"I guess I'm late again," said Willy. "It's funny that I'm always late. I wish I could get to school on time every day."

What should Willy do to get to school on time every day?
Do you think Willy will start getting to school on time every day? Why not?

Willy never thought to start earlier.

When Willy finally got to school, his teacher said, "Willy, I wish you'd get to school on time."

"I'm glad to hear that," said Willy. "With both of us wishing, maybe it will happen."

Do you think that Willy's teacher was really helping Willy wish so that he would get to school on time?

6　**Willy the Wisher**

The Thing That Went Under the Door

One day when Ferdie and Portia were watching TV, they saw something run across the floor and under the door. It was going so fast they didn't see what it was, and when they opened the door to look, it was gone.

"I wonder what that was that ran under the door," said Portia.

"I don't know," said Ferdie. "Maybe it was a dog."

**Was that a good guess?
Could it have been a dog?
Why not?**

"Maybe it was a little fish," said Portia.

**Was that a good guess?
Could it have been a fish?
Why not?**

"No," said Ferdie, "I think it was a bird."

**Was that a good guess?
Could it have been a bird?
Why not?**

"I think it was a worm," said Portia.

What do you think it could have been? [Discuss the possibilities.]

Well, Ferdie and Portia never found out for sure what it was, because they never saw it again. But they decided that it was something big and slow.

Do you think they were right?

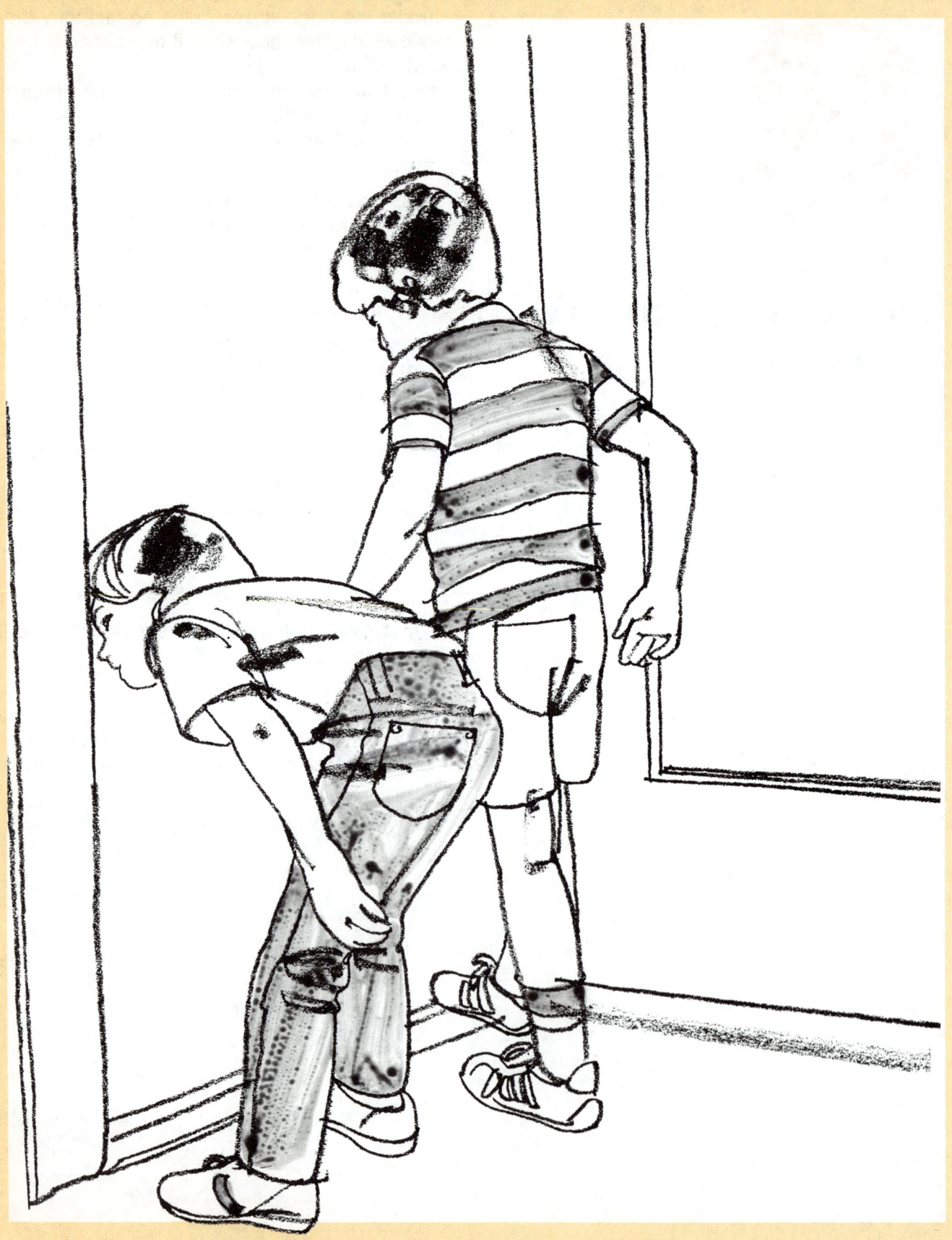

8   **The Thing That Went Under the Door**

4

Something Green for Mrs. Nosho

Mrs. Nosho works in a big department store. She has so many things to do that she has a special room to work in and a boy named Phil to help her. Phil tries very hard to do what Mrs. Nosho wants, but it isn't always easy. "The trouble is," says Phil, "that when Mrs. Nosho tells me what she wants, I still don't know what she wants."

One day Mrs. Nosho had a big pile of old papers and letters that she wanted to get rid of, so she called Phil into her office.

"Phil, I don't want these old papers and letters any more. Will you please take them somewhere?" asked Mrs. Nosho.

Phil picked up the old papers and letters and took them outside and started to put them in the mailbox.

Was that the place to put those old letters and papers?
Did Mrs. Nosho tell Phil enough?
What should Mrs. Nosho have told Phil?

Mrs. Nosho came running outside. "Phil! Not in the mailbox! Throw them in the trash!"

"Oh, I didn't know," said Phil.

How could Phil have found out?

"Then you should ask me a question," said Mrs. Nosho.

What question should Phil ask Mrs. Nosho?

"I see," said Phil. "Where do I put these old papers and letters?"

"In the trash, please," said Mrs. Nosho.

Later Mrs. Nosho called Phil in to get rid of a bucket of water that the window washers had left in her office.

"Phil, please get rid of that dirty water," she said.

Phil picked up the bucket and poured the water all over the floor.

Was that the place to get rid of the water?

"Oh, dear!" shouted Mrs. Nosho. "Not on the floor. Pour it where it's supposed to go."

"But I don't know where it's supposed to go," said Phil.

How could Phil have found out?

"Remember, if you don't know, ask a question," said Mrs. Nosho.

What should Phil ask Mrs. Nosho?

"Where should I pour the dirty water, Mrs. Nosho?" asked Phil.
"In the sink," said Mrs. Nosho.

"Oh, by the way, Phil," said Mrs. Nosho, "my desk is dusty. Please get something to clean it with."
Phil brought back a wet mop and mopped the top of the desk, papers and all.

Was that what Mrs. Nosho wanted Phil to clean the desk with?
What should she have told Phil?

"A wet mop won't work, Phil," said Mrs. Nosho.
"I didn't know that," said Phil.
"Remember, if you don't know, ask a question," said Mrs. Nosho.

What could Phil ask to find out?

"All right," said Phil. "What should I use to clean the desk with?"
"I think a cloth would do the job nicely," said Mrs. Nosho.

"One more thing, Phil," said Mrs. Nosho. "My office is awfully dreary. Could you get something green for the office so it will be prettier?"
Phil rushed right out and got a basket full of pretty green frogs and let them loose in Mrs. Nosho's office.

Do you think Mrs. Nosho wanted frogs?
What do you think she wanted?

Frogs were jumping all over the place, and Mrs. Nosho was jumping up and down too.
"Don't let those frogs jump all over the office!" shouted Mrs. Nosho.
"Where should I put them?" asked Phil.

Mrs. Nosho looked surprised. "You asked a question! You're learning fast, Phil. Take them back where they came from. And then I still need something green."

Should Phil ask another question?
What question should he ask?

"What do you want that's green, Mrs. Nosho?" asked Phil.
"I'd like a plant in a pot, please," Mrs. Nosho told him.

When Phil came back with the plant, Mrs. Nosho said, "Would you please get me some coffee too?"
Phil came back with a bucket of coffee.

Do you think Mrs. Nosho wanted a whole bucket of coffee?
How much coffee do you think she wanted?

"Not that much coffee!" said Mrs. Nosho.
"I'm sorry, Mrs. Nosho," said Phil. "I just didn't know."
"Then ask a question, Phil," said Mrs. Nosho.

What should Phil ask Mrs. Nosho?

"How much coffee do you want, Mrs. Nosho?" asked Phil.
"Just one cup, please," said Mrs. Nosho. "Would you get me a cup?"

"When you've brought the coffee, you can go somewhere," said Mrs. Nosho.

Should Phil ask a question now?
What should he ask?

Phil thought a minute, then asked, "Where do you want me to go, Mrs. Nosho?"
"Oh, you may go home, Phil," said Mrs. Nosho. "You've done enough work today."

5

Ferdie and the Pot

Ferdie is very smart. He knows a lot of things and he thinks a lot. The trouble with Ferdie is that he thinks he knows everything and that everything he says is true. He tells everybody that he *never* says anything that is not true. Now that's pretty hard to do, even for Ferdie.

One day Ferdie's grandfather was standing by the stove, stirring something in a big blue pot. Ferdie came in to watch him. Grandfather decided to play a little trick on Ferdie, to teach him a lesson. "Do you still think that everything you say is true, Ferdie?" he asked.

"Yes, I do," said Ferdie.

"Let's play a little game," said Grandfather. "You tell me everything about this big blue pot that I'm stirring, and we'll see if everything you say is true."

"That's an easy game," said Ferdie. "I know all about that pot, and everything I tell you will be true. First, it's a pot."

Is that true?

"Good," said Grandfather. "That's true. Tell me some more."

"It's blue," said Ferdie.

Is that true?

"Tell me more," said Grandfather.

"It's big," said Ferdie.

Is that true?

"Tell me more," said Grandfather.

"It's on the stove," said Ferdie.

Is that true?

"Tell me more," said Grandfather.

"It's hot," said Ferdie.

Why did Ferdie say it's hot?

"Tell me more," said Grandfather. "Tell me about what's in the pot."

Ferdie looked in the pot and saw a yellowish liquid with things floating in it. "There's soup in that pot," said Ferdie.

Ferdie and the Pot 13

Why did Ferdie think there was soup in the pot?

"You told me that it's a pot and that it's blue and that it's big and that it's on the stove," said Grandfather. "All of those things are true. But you also told me that it's hot."

"Of course it is," said Ferdie, "because it's on the stove."

"Well, feel the pot," said Grandfather.

Ferdie touched the pot carefully, so he wouldn't burn himself. But the pot wasn't even warm. "Why, it's cold!" said Ferdie.

How could the pot be cold, even though it's on the stove?

"Now taste what's in the pot," said Grandfather. He took a spoon and dipped out a little of the yellowish liquid and let Ferdie taste it.

"Why, this doesn't taste like soup," said Ferdie. "It tastes like lemonade!"

Then Ferdie looked more closely and saw that the things that were floating in the pot were ice cubes.

Were all the things that Ferdie said about the pot true?
What things did he say that were not true?

"Most of the things you told me were true," said Grandfather. "But not all of them."

"Well, they should have been true," said Ferdie, who was a little angry at being wrong. "The pot should have been hot and it should have had soup in it. Who ever heard of making lemonade on a stove!"

Why might Grandfather have been making lemonade on the stove?

"Perhaps you're right," said Grandfather. "But the pot is so big that I didn't have any place else to put it. If you're always going to say things that are true, you're going to have to learn that things are not always the way you think they're supposed to be."

6

Willy and Mrs. Nosho

Willy often goes for walks with Mrs. Nosho. Mrs. Nosho is always telling Willy about something or other, but Willy can never tell just what Mrs. Nosho is talking about.

One Sunday, Willy and Mrs. Nosho were walking along and Mrs. Nosho said, "Willy, I used to live in that house." And she waved a hand at all the houses on the block.

Willy thought, "I wish I knew which house she is talking about."

Can Willy find out by wishing?
How can he find out?
What question could he ask to find out which house Mrs. Nosho means?

"*Which* house did you live in?" asked Willy.
"That one," said Mrs. Nosho, and she waved her hand at *all* the houses again.

Willy thought, "It didn't help enough to ask that question. All the houses look the same to me. I wish I knew which house she used to live in."

Do all the houses look the same to you? [Show the illustration on page 16.]
How are they different?
What could Willy ask to find out what he wants to know?

"What color is the house?" asked Willy.
"It's the white one," said Mrs. Nosho.

Did Willy find out?
How did he find out?

They walked a little farther and came to two trees. Mrs. Nosho said, "I've always liked that tree," and she waved at both trees.

Willy thought, "I wish I knew which tree she likes. If I ask 'Which one?,' she'll just say 'That one.' I wish I knew which one. They're both trees and they look alike to me. I can't tell which tree she likes."

Do the trees look alike to you? [Show the illustration.]
How are the trees different?
What should Willy do to find out which tree Mrs. Nosho likes?
What question could he ask?

16 Willy and Mrs. Nosho

"Is it the tall tree, Mrs. Nosho?" asked Willy.

Could Mrs. Nosho say yes?
Could Mrs. Nosho say no?
Will Willy find out which tree it is?

"No," said Mrs. Nosho, "it's not the tall tree."
"That's too bad," Willy said to himself. "Now I still don't know which tree she likes. I wish I knew."

Does Willy need to ask another question?
Can you figure out which tree Mrs. Nosho likes *without* asking another question? (Yes. She likes the short one.)

Willy thought hard. "There are only two trees," he thought. "I know it's not the tall tree, so it must be the short tree!"
"Oh, I know now," said Willy, "it's the short tree!"
"Right!" said Mrs. Nosho. "I like that short tree."

They came to a park. "Say, there's my brother's dog over there," said Mrs. Nosho, and she waved a hand at four dogs playing in the grass.
Willy thought, "I know I should ask a question. I just wish I knew what to ask."

What would you ask?

Willy thought and thought some more. "Let me see, some of the dogs are white and some of the dogs are black . . ."

Is Willy thinking or wishing? [Show the illustration.] What could he ask? What else?

"Is your brother's dog black?" asked Willy.
"No," said Mrs. Nosho. "His dog is not black. His dog is white."

Does Willy know which dog it is yet?
Why not?

"Which white one is it?" asked Willy.

What do you think Mrs. Nosho will say?

"That one," said Mrs. Nosho, and she waved her hand at all the dogs again. Willy wished and wished that he knew which white dog belonged to Mrs. Nosho's brother.

How can Willy find out which white dog belongs to Mrs. Nosho's brother?
How are the white dogs different from each other?
What could Willy ask?

Willy thought and thought and finally asked, "Mrs. Nosho, does your brother's white dog have a long tail?" Willy said to himself, "Now I'll know for sure."
"No," said Mrs. Nosho, "his dog does not have a long tail. But his dog is white."

Can Willy tell which dog it is now?
Can you tell?

"I like his dog," said Willy. "I like white dogs with short tails."

When they came back from their walk, Mrs. Nosho said, "You really asked a lot of questions, Willy."
Willy said, "I wish I didn't have to ask so many questions, but I do."
"That's all right," said Mrs. Nosho. "People usually ask me a lot of questions. I don't know why."

Why do people ask Mrs. Nosho so many questions?

Willy and Mrs. Nosho

7

Poor Old Bowser

The Noshos' big dog, Bowser, was very, very unhappy . . .

You don't know why he was unhappy, do you? If you want to know, you'll have to ask me a question.

Bowser was unhappy because he caused some big trouble around the house . . .

Ask me a question about the trouble.

Bowser broke some things that the Noshos liked very much . . .

Now what can you ask me?

He broke their best dishes, but he did it in a funny way . . .

What can you ask me now?

He was running around a little table, chasing something . . .

You don't know what he was chasing, do you? Ask me.

He was chasing his own tail around the little table, and something happened . . .

Now what can you ask me?

He tripped and knocked over the table. There were dishes on the table, and all the dishes fell off and broke. Mr. Nosho was so cross that he did something really awful to poor old Bowser . . .

What can you ask me now?

Mr. Nosho made Bowser stay outside and wouldn't give him his very favorite thing . . .

Now what can you ask?

He wouldn't give him a bone!

Now you know what happened to poor old Bowser. What did you have to do to find out?

Poor Old Bowser 19

The Woman with the Wood

One day Ferdie and Portia saw a woman carrying wood into the garage of the house across the street. Then she took in a saw, a hammer, and some nails and closed the door. They could hear her sawing and hammering, but they couldn't see what she was doing.

"I wonder what she's making," said Portia.

"I'll bet she's making a bicycle," said Ferdie.

Is that a good guess?
Why not?

"She can't be making a bicycle," said Portia. "A bicycle isn't made of wood."

"Well then, she's probably building a fireplace," said Ferdie.

Is that a good guess?
Why not?

"She'd need stones or bricks for a fireplace," said Portia.

"You could make a fireplace out of just wood if you didn't have any bricks or stones," said Ferdie.

What would happen to a fireplace made of wood when you lit a fire?

"No," said Portia. "The fireplace would burn up."

"Maybe she's making a dress," Portia went on.

Is that a good guess?
Why not?

"Don't be silly," said Ferdie. "Dresses aren't made of wood."

"Well, I suppose she might be making a stand for a TV," Portia said.

"That's a bad guess," said Ferdie. "She wouldn't have a TV in the garage."

Do you think Portia made a bad guess?
Could you make a TV stand in the garage and take it into the house?

Can you think of any reason why someone might build a TV stand in the garage instead of doing it in the living room?

"She could make a TV stand in the garage and then take it inside," said Portia. "Maybe she doesn't want to hammer inside the house."

Ferdie said, "Well, I still think it's not a TV stand, but I can't think of anything else it could be."

Can you think of anything else it could be?

Finally Ferdie said, "I'm going to ask her what she's making and show you that you're wrong about the TV stand, Portia."

Ferdie went across the street and yelled through the garage door, "Could you please tell me what you're making with all that wood?"

The woman with the wood said, "I don't speak English."

So Ferdie and Portia never did find out.

Can you think of any other way Portia and Ferdie might have found out what the woman was making?

The Woman with the Wood

Would You Rather Have the Dog?

Ferdie likes to help his friends. And Ferdie's friends often ask him to help them. One day Ferdie's teacher asked him to help her. "Ferdie," she said, "will you please help me make our bulletin board look nice? Go and get the things we'll need."

Ferdie wasn't sure about what to get. "What do we need?" he asked.

"You can figure that out, Ferdie," said his teacher. "What do you have to think about to make a nice bulletin board? Just think about the things we'll need and go get them."

What would you get to make a bulletin board look nice?

Ferdie thought a little while. Then he brought some pictures of boys and girls playing in the snow.

Will they help make the bulletin board look nice?
Why or why not?

Ferdie thought of more things to bring. He wasn't sure that all the things would help, but he brought them anyway.

Ferdie brought some cookies.

Will they help the bulletin board look nice?
Why or why not?

Ferdie brought some tacks.

Will they help make the board look nice?
How?

Ferdie brought a pencil.

Will that help?
How?

Ferdie brought a long, long piece of red ribbon.

Will that help make the board look nice?
Why or why not?

Ferdie brought a picture that he had drawn.

Will that help?
Why or why not?

And Ferdie brought a table.

**Will that help make the board look nice?
Why or why not?**

Ferdie loves to help his mother cook.
One day Ferdie's mother said, "Ferdie, will you please help me fix breakfast? Go and get the things we'll need."
Ferdie wasn't sure what to get. "What do we need?" he asked.
"You can figure that out, Ferdie," his mother said. "What do you have to think about when you want to cook breakfast? Just think about the things you'll need and go and get them."
Ferdie thought a little. Then he brought his mother some eggs.

**Will they help Ferdie and his mother make breakfast? How?
What would you bring to help someone make breakfast?**

Ferdie thought some more and brought more things to his mother.
Ferdie brought his snowsuit.

**Will that help with breakfast?
Why or why not?**

Ferdie brought some plates.

**Will they help?
Why or why not?**

Ferdie brought a pancake turner.

**Will it help?
How?**

Ferdie brought the dog.

**Will it help?
Why or why not?**

Ferdie brought three oranges.

**Will they help with breakfast?
How?**

Ferdie brought his toy truck.

**Will it help with breakfast?
Why or why not?**

After breakfast Ferdie's mother called him outside. "Ferdie," she said, "there's a big hole in the roof of the garage that has to be fixed right away! The man who takes care of our apartment building is away, so will you please help me fix it? Go and get the things we'll need."
Ferdie didn't know what to get. "What will we need?" he asked.
"You can figure that out, Ferdie," said his mother. "What do you have to think about when you want to fix a hole in the garage roof? Just think about the things we'll need and get them."

What would you bring to help fix a hole in the garage roof?

Ferdie thought and thought. Then he brought his mother the cat.

**Will it help fix the hole in the roof?
Why or why not?**

Then Ferdie brought a lot of other things to his mother.
Ferdie brought an ax.

**Will it help fix the hole in the garage roof?
Why or why not?**

Ferdie brought a bucket of water.

**Will it help fix the hole in the roof?
Why or why not?**

Ferdie brought some nails.

**Will they help fix the hole in the roof?
How?**

Ferdie brought some boards.

**Will they help fix the roof?
How?**

Ferdie brought his mittens.

**Will they help fix the roof?
Why or why not?**

Ferdie brought his bathing suit.

Will it help?
Why or why not?

Ferdie brought a hammer.

Will it help?
How?

Ferdie brought a ladder.

Will it help fix a hole in the garage roof?
How?

When Ferdie's mother looked at all the things Ferdie had brought, she said, "You brought a lot of things, Ferdie. Some of these will help fix the roof and some of them won't. I really wonder why you brought the cat."

"I don't know," said Ferdie. "Would you rather have the dog?"

Does it make any difference whether Ferdie brought a cat or a dog?
Why not?

10

The House Where Sleeby Dwells

Mr. Sleeby lives in a big house all by himself. He doesn't take very good care of his house; when things get broken, he just leaves them that way and forgets about them. He doesn't fix things because he forgets that they are broken.

One day Mr. Sleeby's cousin, George, came to visit. Cousin George didn't know that so many things were broken at Mr. Sleeby's house, or he might not have come. When he walked up to the front door, he pushed the doorbell button. Mr. Sleeby was home, but he didn't answer the door because he didn't hear the doorbell.

**Did Cousin George push the doorbell button?
Why didn't Mr. Sleeby answer the door?**

"I guess the bell isn't working," thought Cousin George. "I'll knock."

Cousin George knocked very hard, and Mr. Sleeby poked his head out the window. "Come on in," he said, "the door's not locked."

Cousin George couldn't even start to open the door. And it didn't really matter if it was locked or not.

What do you think is wrong with the door?

Cousin George shouted, "I can't open your door. There's no doorknob. Come down and let me in."

Mr. Sleeby came down and opened the door. The inside doorknob came off in his hand. "H'm," he said, "I'll have to remember to fix that doorknob." He set the doorknob down on the floor in the hall.

**Do you think Mr. Sleeby will remember to fix the doorknob?
Why or why not?**

"You can take your suitcase upstairs to the bedroom," said Mr. Sleeby. "Put your suitcase on the chair and put your clothes in the dresser drawers. They're empty."

Cousin George went up to the bedroom and put his suitcase on the chair, but something was wrong. He had to bend down near the floor to open his suitcase.

What do you think is wrong with that chair? (no legs)

Cousin George took his clothes out of the suitcase and put them in the top drawer of the dresser, just as Mr. Sleeby had told him to do. He heard things falling. He looked down, and all his clothes were on the floor in front of the dresser.

How did that happen? (no bottom in any of the drawers)

Cousin George didn't get angry. He just picked up his clothes and set them on top of the dresser.

Then he went into the bathroom to wash his hands, but he couldn't turn on the water in the sink. The faucet was there, but he couldn't turn it on.

What do you think is wrong?

He shouted down to Mr. Sleeby, "The faucets on your sink don't have any handles on them."

"I forgot about that," said Mr. Sleeby. "You'll have to wash your hands in the bathtub until I get those faucets fixed."

Do you think Mr. Sleeby will really fix the faucets?
Why not?

Cousin George shrugged his shoulders. The faucet in the bathtub had no handles either. But it was leaking enough so that he could wash his hands under it anyway.

Cousin George went down to the living room. He decided to sit down in a chair and read a book. He found a chair that wasn't too bad, although it had no back. But when he turned on the lamp, the light shone in his eyes so much that he couldn't read.

What do you think is wrong with the lamp?

"I can't read by your lamp," said Cousin George. "It doesn't have a shade."

"There's a shade for it someplace," said Mr. Sleeby. "But I can't remember where I put it."

Where is a good place to keep a lampshade so you'll have it when you need it? (on the lamp)

Cousin George said, "Oh, well, if I can't read, I'll just lie down on the couch and rest." He took one look at the couch and shouted, "I can't rest on your couch. It will be too hard."

What do you think is wrong with the couch? (no cushions)

"That's funny," said Mr. Sleeby. "I remember that couch being very soft."

Does Mr. Sleeby know what's wrong with the couch?

"I think I'll go upstairs and fix a few things for you," said Mr. Sleeby. "Why don't you get yourself something to eat?"

Cousin George found some bread and some cheese, but he needed a knife. There was only one knife, and he couldn't use it. "If I try to use this knife," he said, "I'll cut my hand."

What do you think is wrong with the knife? (no handle)

Instead of cutting the bread and cheese, Cousin George just broke off pieces and ate them.

"You can come upstairs now," shouted Mr. Sleeby. "I've fixed things for you."

Do you think Mr. Sleeby fixed the chair?
Do you think he fixed the dresser or the faucets in the bathroom? Why not?

When Cousin George got upstairs, he found that the chair still had no legs and the faucets in the bathroom still had no handles. "I don't see that you've done anything," he said.

"Yes, I have," said Mr. Sleeby. "I noticed that you left your clothes on top of the dresser, so I put them in a drawer for you."

The House Where Sleeby Dwells

**Will Cousin George find his clothes in the drawer? Why not?
Where will he find them?**

Cousin George picked his clothes off the floor and put them back in his suitcase. "I can't stay here any longer," he told Mr. Sleeby. "I'll come back when you get everything fixed." Then he walked to the front door.

Will Cousin George be able to get out? Why not?

Cousin George couldn't open the front door because it had no doorknob. He looked around for some other way to get out of the house.

Can you think of other ways he could get out of the house?

Cousin George went out by the back door, which was a screen door. It didn't have a doorknob either, but it also didn't have a screen.

How could Cousin George get out through that door if it didn't have a doorknob?

"I hope you'll come back and visit me after I get my house fixed up," said Mr. Sleeby.
"I will," said Cousin George.

Do you think that Cousin George will ever come back to visit?

"Don't forget," said Mr. Sleeby.

11

How Mr. Sleeby's House Got That Way

Remember all the things that were wrong with Mr. Sleeby's house?

Why couldn't Cousin George open Mr. Sleeby's front door? (no doorknob)
Why did Cousin George step through Mr. Sleeby's back door? (no doorknob, no screen)
Why couldn't Cousin George wash his hands in the sink? (no handles on the faucets)
What was wrong with Mr. Sleeby's chair? (no legs)
Why was Mr. Sleeby's couch uncomfortable? (no cushions)
What was wrong with the knife? (no handle)
Why did Cousin George's clothes fall down when he put them in the dresser? (no drawer bottoms)
How did Mr. Sleeby's lamp keep Cousin George from reading? (The light shone in his eyes because the lamp had no shade.)

Would you like to know how Mr. Sleeby's house got that way?

Well, one day Mr. Sleeby went out his front door to bring in the paper. He turned the doorknob and pulled, and the door opened easily. [Demonstrate.] But the door shut behind him. When he wanted to go back inside, he tugged on the doorknob but the door didn't open.
"That's funny," said Mr. Sleeby. "I'm pulling very hard, but the door doesn't move." [Demonstrate.]

Should Mr. Sleeby keep pulling on the doorknob to get in?
What other things could he try? (turning the knob, pushing, or using a key, for instance)

Mr. Sleeby kept pulling harder and harder from the outside.

What do you think happened? [Demonstrate with a door, having a child do what Mr. Sleeby did.]

Finally the doorknob came off in Mr. Sleeby's hand.

31

32 How Mr. Sleeby's House Got That Way

"I'll try the back door," said Mr. Sleeby. He went around to the screen door in back and pulled on its knob. The screen door didn't open either. He pulled harder and harder until finally that doorknob came off in his hand too.

"Oh, well," said Mr. Sleeby, "I'll just have to take out the screen." He took out the screen and crawled through the door.

Will Mr. Sleeby remember to put the screen back in the door?
Why should he put the screen back in the door?

That's how Mr. Sleeby's doors lost their doorknobs and the screen door lost its screen.

One day when Mr. Sleeby was in his bathroom he said, "Say, I'll bet these faucet handles will make good doorknobs." So he took the faucet handles off the sink and the bathtub and tried to put them on the doors downstairs.

Will faucet handles work to fix those doors? Why not?

"These don't fit," said Mr. Sleeby, so he threw the faucet handles into the bushes.

What should Mr. Sleeby have done with those faucet handles?

That's how Mr. Sleeby's faucets lost their handles.

Later Mr. Sleeby went into the bedroom and sat down in a chair. The chair swayed a little as he sat in it. Mr. Sleeby started to rock back and forth, farther and farther.

"That's funny," said Mr. Sleeby, "I didn't know this is a rocking chair. It doesn't have any rockers either."

Is it a rocking chair?
Why is it rocking back and forth? (The legs are loose.)

The chair went back and forth, back and forth, back and forth, because Mr. Sleeby was having fun rocking. Then, wham! Mr. Sleeby was on the floor.

What happened?

The legs had broken off.
"I guess it wasn't really a rocking chair after all," said Mr. Sleeby.

That's how the chair in the bedroom lost its legs.

The next time Mr. Sleeby tried to sit in the chair without legs, he noticed that it was very low. "This is almost like sitting on the floor," he said. "I'll have to pile some cushions on this chair."

Where do you think Mr. Sleeby got the cushions?

He took the seat cushions from the couch in the living room and piled them on the chair without legs.

Is that a good way to make the chair higher? Why or why not?

Then Mr. Sleeby tried to sit on top of all those cushions, but they were too tippy and he kept falling off.

"These don't work," said Mr. Sleeby. So he took the cushions off the chair and piled them in the corner of the bedroom.

What should he have done with those cushions?

That's how Mr. Sleeby's couch lost its cushions.

One day Mr. Sleeby was cutting a ham with a knife. There was a big bone through the middle of the ham, but he didn't think about that.

"My, this ham is hard to cut," he said. "I thought it was easy at first, but now I can't cut it at all."

Why can't Mr. Sleeby cut through the ham? What did he forget?

How Mr. Sleeby's House Got That Way

Mr. Sleeby pushed harder and harder on the knife. Suddenly he heard a cracking sound, and then he couldn't cut any more.

What happened to the knife? (The handle broke off.)

"I guess I won't cut any more ham today," said Mr. Sleeby, "if it's going to ruin my knife that way."

That's how Mr. Sleeby's knife lost its handle.

Mr. Sleeby liked to have a fire in the fireplace when it was cold, so he bought some logs. He decided to keep them in the drawers of a dresser, but they were a little too big and the drawers wouldn't close.

What do you think Mr. Sleeby did to the drawers?

"I know," said Mr. Sleeby, "I'll take the bottoms out of the drawers, and then the logs won't get stuck."

Is the dresser a good place to keep logs? Why not?
Is it a good idea to take the bottoms out of the drawers? Why not?

Mr. Sleeby took the bottoms out of the drawers and put them beside the dresser.

Do you think he'll remember to put them back?

Then Mr. Sleeby was able to get the logs into the dresser. He was very pleased about that. But in the winter, when he burned the logs in the fireplace, he forgot and burned the bottoms of the dresser drawers, too. So when summer came, all he had left was an empty dresser with no bottoms in the drawers.

One night Mr. Sleeby wanted to read, but it was too dark. When he tried to turn on the lamp, the light didn't go on.

What could be wrong?

"Maybe the bulb is burned out," he said.

He took off the lampshade and put in a new bulb.

Then the lamp worked, but the light was so bright it hurt his eyes.

Why? What had Mr. Sleeby forgotten to do?

"I know," he said at last. "I need a lampshade."

He got the lampshade and put it on his head. It came down to his chin.

"That's a lot better," he said. "Now there's no light in my eyes, but I still can't read."

Why can't Mr. Sleeby read?

Mr. Sleeby took the lampshade off his head and put it behind the couch.

What should Mr. Sleeby have done?

That's how Mr. Sleeby's lamp lost its shade.

Mr. Sleeby gave up trying to read. He tried to lie down on the couch, but it was too hard. He tried to take a bath, but the faucets wouldn't work. He tried to cut himself some meat, but the knife hurt his hand.

"I guess I'll go to bed," said Mr. Sleeby, "and try again tomorrow."

What do you think Mr. Sleeby might try to do tomorrow?
What would you do to help Mr. Sleeby?

The Shovel in the Basement

Ferdie and Portia saw a man go into the basement of their apartment building, carrying a shovel.

"What do you think he's going to do?" asked Portia.

"I think he's going to kill rats with that shovel," said Ferdie.

**Is that a good guess?
Could you kill a rat with a shovel?
Is that a way people would try to get rid of rats in a basement?**

"Wouldn't he use traps to kill rats?" asked Portia.

"He could use traps," said Ferdie, "but he could do it with a shovel, too."

"I don't think he could run fast enough," said Portia.

"Well, maybe he's going to make a garden down there," said Ferdie.

**Is that a good guess? Why not?
Why don't people plant gardens in basements?**

"I think a garden needs lots of sun," said Portia.

"The basement has windows," said Ferdie.

"Not very many," said Portia. "Anyway, I've been down in the basement, and I know it has a cement floor. You can't grow flowers in cement."

"Maybe he's just going to use the shovel to make a hole in the cement," Portia suggested.

**Is that a good guess?
Could you make a hole in concrete with something as light as a shovel?**

"Why would he want to make a hole in the floor?" said Ferdie. "I think he's going to shovel snow with that shovel."

**Is that a good guess?
Why not?**

"It's not snowing," said Portia.

36 **The Shovel in the Basement**

"Not up here," said Ferdie, "but maybe in the basement."

Could it be snowing in the basement?

Portia laughed and said, "Ferdie, you know that's not so good." Then she said, "Maybe he wants to hide the shovel."

Is that a good guess?

"Well, maybe," said Ferdie, "but most people don't hide the tools they need to do things."

They tried really hard, but they couldn't think of any other reason why the man would take a shovel to the basement.

Can you?

13

Portia's Birthday

"Your birthday is tomorrow, Portia," said Ferdie. "What would you like?"

"If I tell you what I'd like, I won't be surprised," said Portia. "I don't care what I get, just so it's a surprise."

"That should be easy," said Ferdie, and he went off by himself to try to think of a surprise.

The next day he brought her a big red box.

"Oh, boy," she said, "it's something big." She opened it, but she still didn't know what her present was.

Why do you think she still didn't know what her present was?

Inside the big red box was a blue box.

"It must be inside the blue box," said Portia. She opened the blue box, but she still didn't know.

Why do you think she still didn't know what her present was?

Inside the blue box was a smaller red box.

What do you think she found inside the red box?

Inside the red box was a smaller blue box.

What do you think she found inside the blue box? [Continue the pattern until all the children are predicting successfully; then use the following ending.]

Inside the blue box was a tiny, tiny red box about this big. [Indicate between two and three centimeters.]

"I'll bet I know what's inside this little red box," said Portia. "A little blue box."

But when she opened the red box, she didn't find a blue box at all. She found a penny. And with the penny was a note, all folded up. The note said, "When I finished buying the boxes, this penny was all I had left. Happy birthday! Ferdie."

"It's a surprise, all right," said Portia, "but I don't know what I'll do with all these boxes." Then she thought, "I know. When it's Ferdie's birthday, I'll give these boxes to Ferdie for a surprise."

Will it be a surprise if Portia gives those same boxes to Ferdie for his birthday?
Why or why not?

Mark Wraps a Present

Mark was going to a birthday party for Portia.

"I want to take her a present," said Mark. "What do I do?"

"I'll tell you," said his mother. "You just have to do four things. First you buy a present. Then you put it in a box. Then you wrap paper around the box. Then you tie the box with a ribbon. Can you remember those four things?"

"I'll try," said Mark.

Let's help Mark remember. What should he do first?
Then what should he do?
What's next?
What's the last thing?

Now here's what Mark did. First he bought a book. Then he wrapped paper around a box. Then he tied it with a ribbon.

Did he remember everything? [If the children spot the missing step, ask them what they think will happen. Otherwise go on.]

Mark took the present to Portia.

She said, "My, what a pretty present!" She untied the ribbon, unwrapped the paper, and opened the box.

Guess what she found in the box. (She didn't find anything in the box. It was empty.)
Why was it empty? What did Mark forget?

The next week Ferdie had a birthday, and Mark was going to take him a present.

"This time I'm going to do it right," said Mark.

He bought Ferdie a shiny white jet plane with wings and a tail that were sharp and with a point that stuck out in front. Then he wrapped paper around it and tied it with a ribbon.

Did Mark forget anything?
What do you think will happen?

"Will Ferdie ever be surprised to get this present!" said Mark.

He handed the present to Ferdie and said, "You'll never guess what this is."

Ferdie said, "Oh, boy! A white jet plane!"

"How do you know?" Mark asked.

How do you think Ferdie could tell it was a jet plane before he unwrapped it?
How did he know it was white?

"It was easy," said Ferdie. "Here's a white wing sticking out through the paper, and here's another white wing sticking out, and here's the tail sticking out, and here's a point sticking out in front. It must be a jet plane."

What did Mark forget?

"I forgot the box," said Mark unhappily. "If I'd put it in a box, you wouldn't have guessed what it was."

Was Mark right?
Could Ferdie have guessed what it was?
What might Ferdie have guessed it was?

"Yes, I would," said Ferdie. "I'd have guessed it was a box."

15

I Forgot What You Needed

Ferdie was visiting his grandfather's farm. Grandfather had promised Ferdie a rabbit if Ferdie would help him make a rabbit hutch to keep it in.

"The first thing we need to do," said Grandfather, "is to make a list of all the things we need for the hutch. Let's see—wood, screen, tacks, paint . . . But I'll forget all this if I don't write it down. I have a pencil but no paper. Ferdie, please run into the house and get me the paper."

Ferdie ran into the house and came back with a newspaper.

Is that what Grandfather wanted?
What did Ferdie forget?

"I forgot you needed paper to write on," said Ferdie. "I'll get some."

After Grandfather made his list, he began to work on the hutch. He made the framework and started to tack screen on it.

"Oh, my," he said, "this box of tacks is empty. Ferdie, would you run to the storeroom and get me a new box, please?"

Ferdie found the storeroom and saw a lot of boxes of different sizes.

"Here's a nice-looking new box," he said to himself. "Maybe Grandfather would like this one."

He took the nice empty box to Grandfather.

Is that what Grandfather wanted?
What did Ferdie forget?

"I forgot you needed tacks," said Ferdie. "I'll get a box with tacks in it."

A little later, Grandfather was ready to paint. "I brought out the paint, Ferdie," he said, "but I forgot the brush. Would you go back to the house and get me a brush?"

What might Ferdie have come back with?

Ferdie went back to the house, trying very hard to keep his mind on what he was doing. "Brush," he muttered, "brush, brush."

He came back with a hairbrush.

44 I Forgot What You Needed

**Is that what Grandfather wanted?
What did Ferdie forget?**

"I forgot you needed to paint," said Ferdie. "I'll go get a paintbrush."

Grandfather finished painting and carried the paint can and paintbrush back to the house.

"Oh, my," he said, "I forgot to put the lid back on the paint can. Ferdie, will you run back to where we were painting and get me the lid?"

"Lid," muttered Ferdie as he walked, "lid, lid."

He came back with the lid to the trash can.

**Is that what Grandfather wanted?
What did Ferdie forget?**

"I forgot what kind of lid you needed," said Ferdie. "I'll get the lid to the paint can."

"Guess what!" said Grandfather. "I forgot to make a stand for the rabbit hutch. Please run into the garage and get me a saw. There's one hanging on the wall above the bench."

Ferdie went into the house, thinking "bench, bench." He found a bench in the hall.

Did Ferdie find the saw above that bench?

"Now all I have to remember is what else Grandfather told me," said Ferdie. "Oh, yes, there should be a saw hanging on the wall above the bench. But there isn't. The only thing that's hanging on the wall above the bench is a mirror. Well, maybe that's what he meant."

Ferdie brought the mirror to Grandfather.

**Is that what Grandfather wanted?
What did Ferdie forget?**

"I forgot you said the bench was in the garage," said Ferdie. "I'll find that saw."

Grandfather was measuring the wood for the legs of the stand. "These numbers on the meterstick are pretty small," he said. "Ferdie, you'll find a pair of glasses on the kitchen window sill. Run and get them, please."

What might Ferdie have come back with?

Ferdie ran to the kitchen, saying, "Glasses, glasses. This time I won't forget anything."

He looked around the kitchen and found two drinking glasses.

**Is that what Grandfather wanted?
What did Ferdie forget?**

Ferdie ran back to his grandfather, saying, "I thought of everything this time, Grandfather. I brought two glasses and I even thought to bring us something to drink out of them." He held up a pitcher of lemonade.

Grandfather smiled and wiped the sweat from his forehead. "It isn't exactly what I asked for," he said, "but it *is* exactly what I want. I'm glad to have you for a helper."

Then Ferdie and Grandfather sat down beside the rabbit hutch and drank their lemonade.

16

Mr. Mudanza

Mr. Mudanza liked to change things. Every time he got something new, he changed it into something else.

One day he got a new dresser with five big drawers in it.

Close your eyes and try to get a picture in your mind of Mr. Mudanza's new dresser with five big drawers.

"This is a fine dresser," said Mr. Mudanza, "but I think I'll change it a little."

First he took out the bottom drawer and threw the rest of the dresser away.

Close your eyes if you want to. Can you get a picture in your mind of what that bottom drawer looks like with the rest of the dresser thrown away?

Then he took the knob off the front of the drawer.

Can you picture that drawer with no knob?

The he painted the drawer red.

Now, don't tell me what you think it is yet, but can you picture that—a drawer with no knob and all painted red?

Then Mr. Mudanza put wheels on it, and he put a long, straight handle on one end to pull it with.

Wait . . . Can you picture that—a drawer with no knob and nothing in it, all painted red, with wheels on it and a handle at one end?
Does it still look like a drawer?
What does it look like? (a wagon)
Was that a good thing to do to a new dresser? Why not?

One day Mr. Mudanza got a new floor lamp. It had a long wooden stem and a round wooden bottom. Mr. Mudanza liked his new lamp, but do you think he could leave it the way it was? No. He said, "I think I'll change it a little."

First he took out the light bulb and threw away the lampshade.

46

**Get a picture of the lamp in your mind.
Can you see how it would look with no light bulb and no shade?**

Then he got some sticks and stuck them to the top of the lamp.

Don't tell me what you think it is yet. Can you get a picture in your mind of that lamp with no bulb and no shade, with sticks poking out all over the top?

Then he got a bunch of green leaves and stuck them all over the sticks.

**Can you picture the lamp with sticks poking out and leaves all over the top of it?
Does it look like a lamp any more?
What does it look like (a tree)**

Another day Mr. Mudanza bought a big table. "This is a beautiful table," he said.

Do you think he'll leave the table the way it is?

"But I think I'll change it a little," he said.

Get a picture of that big table in your mind.

First he cut the legs off very short.

Can you picture that big table with the legs cut off short?

Then he covered the tabletop with a big cushion.

Wait . . . Don't say anything yet. Can you picture that table with short legs and a big cushion on top?

Then he threw some sheets and a blanket on top of the cushion.

**Can you see that table with short legs and a big cushion on top, covered with sheets and a blanket?
Does it look like a table any more?
What does it look like? (a bed)**

One day Mr. Mudanza bought himself a big delivery truck, but as soon as he got it home he decided to change it a little.

Do you have a picture of a big truck in your mind?

It was a lot of work changing that truck! First Mr. Mudanza cut a row of square holes along both sides.

Can you see that truck with square holes along both sides?

Then he put windows in all the holes.

Can you see that truck with holes in its sides and windows in all the holes? Wait . . . Don't tell me yet. Wait and make sure you're right.

Then he filled the inside of the truck with seats by all the windows.

**Can you see that truck with lots of windows in its sides and seats by all the windows?
Does it look like a truck any more?
What does it look like? (a bus)**

One day Mr. Mudanza bought a big pot with a lid on it. When he took the pot out of the box, he said, "I think I'll change it a little, although it's a nice pot."

Get a picture of that big pot and lid in your mind.

First he threw away the big pot and kept just the lid.

**What does Mr. Mudanza have now?
Can you picture that lid with no pot?**

Then he took the handle off the top of the lid.

Can you see that big lid without a handle?

Then he turned the lid upside down.

Can you get a picture of that lid without its handle and upside down?

**Does it look like a pot and a lid any more?
What does it look like?** (a plate)
Was that a good thing to do to a new pot? Why not?

Mr. Mudanza still had the big box that the pot came in. "I think I'll change this box a little, too," he said.

First he cut a big square hole in one side and put some wires and things in the box.

Don't say anything yet. Just tell me if you can see that big box with a big square hole in its side.

Then he covered the square hole with glass and put some knobs under the glass.

Can you see that box with a window and some knobs under the window?

Then he stuck a cord with a plug in that box and plugged the cord into the wall.

Can you see that box with a window and some knobs and with a cord plugged into the wall? What does it look like? (a television set)

By the time he had finished changing the box into a television set, Mr. Mudanza was hungry, so he went to get himself an apple. "This is a fine apple," he said, "but I think I'll change it a little." And he changed it into an apple core.

How do you think Mr. Mudanza did that? (He ate the apple.)

Mr. Mudanza 49

17

Manolita Loves Magic

This is Manolita. She loves magic, because she thinks magic makes everything happen. She thinks magic makes cars move, cakes bake, and newspapers appear on the doorstep.

**What do you think makes a car move?
What do you think makes a cake bake?
What do you think makes newspapers appear on the doorstep?
Does magic make those things happen, or do people do something to make them happen?**

Whenever Manolita is asked to do something, she waves her wand and waits for magic to make it happen.

One day Manolita's father, Mr. Mudanza, asked her to change the garden a little so there wouldn't be any weeds. Manolita waved her wand and said, "Weeds, weeds, disappear." But the weeds stayed right there.

**Will magic make those weeds disappear?
How could Manolita make the weeds disappear?**

"You have to pull the weeds out with your hands, Manolita," said Mr. Mudanza.
"Oh, all right," said Manolita.

When Manolita finished pulling out the weeds, Mrs. Mudanza brought her an empty milk bottle and said, "Manolita, we need a quart of milk for lunch."
Manolita waved her wand over the empty milk bottle and said, "Bottle, bottle, fill with milk." But the bottle stayed empty.

**Will magic make that bottle fill with milk?
How could Manolita get a full bottle of milk?**

"You'll have to buy the milk at the store, Manolita," said Mrs. Mudanza. "I left the money for it on the table."
"Oh, all right," said Manolita.

When Manolita got back from the store, she saw that the tire on her bike was soft. She started waving her wand.

How could Manolita make the tire harder?

"Try using the bicycle pump, Manolita," said Mrs. Mudanza.

"Oh, all right," said Manolita, as she pumped up the tire.

"Your shoes are awfully dirty, Manolita," said Mr. Mudanza. "Could you change them a little?"

Manolita tapped them with her wand and said, "Shoes, shoes, shine like the stars." But the shoes were as dirty as ever.

How could Manolita make her shoes shiny?

"The shoe brush is in the closet, Manolita," said Mr. Mudanza. "The polish is there, too."

"Oh, all right," said Manolita, as she went away to brush the dirt off her shoes and to put polish on them.

Out in the kitchen the cat was standing beside its empty food dish, saying, "Meow, meow, meow."

Mr. Mudanza said, "Would you change that empty food dish a little, Manolita, so the cat will stop meowing?"

"I'll change the cat instead," said Manolita. She waved her wand slowly back and forth, right over the cat, and said, "Cat, cat, be quiet as a mouse." But the cat meowed even louder.

What could Manolita do so the cat would stop meowing?

"Try putting cat food in the dish," said Mr. Mudanza.

Manolita did it. And the cat stopped meowing.

Why did that make the cat stop meowing?

"Manolita, it's getting dark in here," said Mrs. Mudanza. "Would you make the room a little lighter?"

Manolita waved her wand and said, "Sun, sun, come out."

Nothing happened.

She waved the wand again and said, "Moon, moon, come out."

Nothing happened.

How could Manolita make the room lighter?

"Try the lamp," said Mrs. Mudanza.

Manolita waved her wand at the lamp, but still nothing happened.

"There's a switch," said Mr. Mudanza.

"Oh, all right," said Manolita. And she switched on the lamp.

"It's getting late, though," said Mr. Mudanza, "and you look tired, Manolita. Would you change yourself a little to make yourself less tired?"

"That's a tough one," said Manolita. "I'll have to think about that one."

What could Manolita do so that she wouldn't be tired any more?

Manolita lay down on the couch and tried to think of some magic to make herself less tired. While she was thinking, she fell asleep.

The next morning she woke up in her own bed. "That's funny," she thought. "I went to sleep on the couch, but now I'm in my own bed. Some magic must have happened while I was asleep."

Do you think it's magic that Manolita went to sleep on the couch and woke up in her own bed?
How do you think it happened?

"You certainly were sleepy last night, Manolita," said Mrs. Mudanza. "You didn't wake up at all when we carried you to bed."

"Oh," said Manolita. "Then it wasn't magic. Too bad. I guess magic just wasn't working yesterday."

Suddenly Manolita remembered how tired she had been when she went to sleep and how hard she had tried to think of some magic to make herself less tired. Now she wasn't tired any more.

"Well," she said, "that's one time my magic really did work."

18

Mrs. Nosho in Her Yard

One very, very hot day, Mrs. Nosho was sitting in her yard.

"I'm hot," she thought. "I'll go get something to drink. That should make me feel better. I don't like feeling so hot!"

She went into the house and fixed herself a big cup of hot coffee.

Will that make Mrs. Nosho feel better? Why not?
What kind of drink does she need? (a cool drink)

Mrs. Nosho went back to the yard. As she drank the coffee, she said to herself, "I don't feel a bit better. I'm still hot! I need something *cool* to drink." So she went into the house and got something cool to drink.

What cool drinks do you know?

A little while later Mrs. Nosho thought, "I think I'll go for a walk in the woods. But I don't have anything on my feet and the ground is rough. I'd better put on something so my feet won't hurt."

She went into her house and put on a pair of socks.

Will socks keep Mrs. Nosho's feet from hurting? Why not?
Does she need to wear something thin on her feet?
What kind of thing should she wear on her feet? (something with tough, thick bottoms)

As she walked down the street, Mrs. Nosho said to herself, "I can feel the rough sidewalk even through these socks. They don't help at all. I need something on my feet that has tough, thick bottoms." So she went back to her house for something else.

What are some things with tough, thick bottoms that Mrs. Nosho could wear on her feet?

As Mrs. Nosho was about to start her walk again, it began to rain. "That rain feels nice and cool," she thought. "I think I'll stay outside even though it's raining. But I don't want to get soaked. I think I'll put a sweater on."

54 Mrs. Nosho in Her Yard

**Will the sweater help her outside in the rain?
Why not?
Would a newspaper over her head help?
What kind of thing does she need?** (something waterproof)

When Mrs. Nosho went outside, she got very wet and so did her sweater. "Oh, dear," she said, "I'm really soaked! If I'm going to stay out here, I'd better put on something that will keep out the water." So she did.

What are some things she could wear that keep out the water when it rains?

After a while it stopped raining, so Mrs. Nosho took some newspapers from the house to read in the yard. The wind started blowing, and Mrs. Nosho's papers flew all over the yard. She ran around the yard and picked them all up.

"H'm," she thought, "I'd better put something on top of these papers so they don't blow away." She went into the house and got another newspaper and put it on top of the other papers.

**Will the newspaper help Mrs. Nosho?
Would a feather keep the papers from blowing away? Why not?
What kind of thing does she need?** (something heavy)

Mrs. Nosho had just sat down again when the top newspaper and all the other papers blew away. "This will never do," she said. "That paper is too light to hold down the other papers. If I want my papers to stay in one place, I'll have to get something heavy to put on top of them. Then they won't blow away."

So she got a heavy piece of ice to put on the papers. Then she sat down to read in the hot sun. The papers didn't blow away any more, but after a while Mrs. Nosho found that something else was wrong with the papers.

What do you think happened to the papers with the piece of ice on them? (They got wet.)

"Those papers are soaking wet," said Mrs. Nosho. "Ah, I see—the ice is melting all over them. I found something to hold the papers down, all right, but now I need to find something to keep the ice from melting."

**Is that really what Mrs. Nosho needs to find?
What kind of thing should she look for that will hold the papers down but not make them wet?** (something heavy and dry)

Mrs. Nosho took away the piece of ice and went looking for something to keep the ice from melting, but she couldn't find anything. When she came back she found that her dog, Bowser, had brought a big, dry bone and set it down on the newspapers.

**Did Bowser help Mrs. Nosho?
How?**

"Good dog, Bowser!" she said. "You've found something just right. It holds the papers down, but it doesn't make them wet."

Bowser wagged his tail happily and ran away with the bone.

"Oh, well," said Mrs. Nosho, "I don't need the bone. Now that I know what *kind* of thing I need to hold the papers down, it will be easy to find something. I can use a rock. I can use a hammer…"

What are some other things Mrs. Nosho could use?

Mrs. Nosho in Her Yard

It's Hard Work to Be a Boss

Mr. Breezy is always telling people what to do. That's his job. He is the boss of dozens of people, and he is always trying to tell them exactly what to do to help them do it right.

Do you think that is an easy job?

It isn't always an easy job for Mr. Breezy.

One morning Mr. Breezy wanted his office boy, Hal, to get some coffee for him. He said, "This is hard, so I'll try to go slow and tell you exactly what to do. You need to go outside, skip to the coffee shop, ask for a cup of coffee, get and pay for the coffee, pick up the coffee, whistle a song, and skip right back to where you started."

Does Hal need to do all those things to get a cup of coffee?
Which things can he forget about?

"I'm sorry," said Hal, "but I'm afraid I can't get your coffee for you."
"Why not?" asked Mr. Breezy.
"Because you told me to whistle a song, and I don't know how to whistle."
"What a shame," said Mr. Breezy. "I know how to whistle, but I can't skip, so I guess I can't get coffee either."

Does someone really need to whistle and skip to get coffee?
Why not?

Later Mr. Breezy needed some letters typed, so he called in his assistant, Terry. "I'll try to make this short," he said, "and I'll try not to forget the important things. Take these letters, run around my desk one time, go to your own desk, get some paper, call your mother on the telephone, and type these letters for me."

Does Terry need to do all those things to type Mr. Breezy's letters?
Which things does she really not need to do?

"I'm sorry," said Terry, "but I'm afraid I can't type your letters for you."
"Dear me, what's wrong?" asked Mr. Breezy.

It's Hard Work to Be a Boss

"Well, you told me to call my mother on the telephone, and I can't do that. My mother doesn't have a telephone."

Mr. Breezy needed those letters typed right away, so he thought and thought and finally he said, "You know, I believe you could type those letters without calling your mother on the telephone."

In the afternoon there was more work to be done. There was a package to be mailed at the post office and there was a delivery truck that needed to be greased. Mr. Breezy called in his helper, Kim, and said, "I have a lot of work for you to do, Kim. I hope this isn't too hard."

"Just tell me slowly," said Kim, "and tell me exactly what to do."

"I'll try," Mr. Breezy said. "Take this package, go out and put it in the delivery truck, drive to the post office, wave at the baker on the street, mail the package at the post office, get back in the truck, eat an apple, take the truck to the garage to be greased, and drive back here."

"That's a lot to do," said Kim, "but I'll try to remember everything."

Does Kim really need to do all those things? Which ones aren't important?

About an hour later Kim came back. "How was your afternoon?" asked Mr. Breezy. "Did you get everything done?"

"I think so," said Kim. "I took the package; I went out and put it in the delivery truck; I drove to the post office; I waved at the baker; I mailed the package at the post office; I got back in the truck; I took the truck to the garage to be greased; and I drove back here."

**Did Kim remember everything that Mr. Breezy told him to do?
What did he forget?**

"You forgot to eat an apple," said Mr. Breezy.

"Sorry," said Kim. "I guess that's why I'm hungry."

Does it matter that Kim forgot to do that?

"I'm hungry too," said Mr. Breezy. "It's hard work being a boss. I have to think so hard to be sure to tell everyone exactly what to do.

"As a matter of fact, I might give up this job and open a school for training dogs instead."

**How could Mr. Breezy make his job easier?
If Mr. Breezy opened a school for training dogs would his job be easier?**

20 First Things First

Mark got out of bed and woke up.

**Does that sound right?
What's wrong with it?
How would you start this story?**

Mark's mother said, "Good! You're up. Be sure to put on a clean shirt this morning."

"All right," said Mark. He put on a clean shirt right away.

"Be sure to take a shower this morning," said Mr. Breezy.

"All right," said Mark. He leaned over the tub and turned on the water.

"Oh, dear!" said Mrs. Breezy. "Now you'll need another clean shirt."

Why will Mark need another clean shirt?

Mark took off his wet shirt. He took a shower and got dressed, putting on another clean shirt.

His mother called upstairs, "I'm going to do a wash this morning. Throw down any clothes that should go in the wash."

"Which clothes should go in?" asked Mark.

"Any clothes you've worn already."

Mark threw the wet shirt downstairs. Then he took off all the clothes he had on and threw them downstairs, too.

**Do you think that's what Mark's mother wanted him to do?
Why did he think she wanted the clothes he had on?**

When he was all dressed (and in his *third* clean shirt), Mark went downstairs.

"Ferdie wants me to call him before school," he said.

He dialed Ferdie's number. Then he took the receiver off the hook and listened for a while.

"He doesn't answer," Mark said.

**Why didn't Ferdie answer?
Do you think Ferdie's phone rang?**

Mark went into the kitchen for breakfast. Mrs. Breezy said, "I made you a hard-boiled egg. It will taste better if you salt it."

59

60   First Things First

Mark shook salt on the hard-boiled egg. Then he took the shell off.

Do you think that's what Mark's mother wanted him to do?
Do you think his egg will taste salty?

Mark's mother said, "Here is a banana you can slice over your cereal."

"I'm having trouble slicing this banana," said Mark. "The knife won't cut through the skin."

What should Mark have done first?

Mrs. Breezy said, "Here's some milk for your cereal. The carton is heavy, so be sure to tip it very slowly."

Mark tipped the milk carton very slowly, until it was almost upside down. Then he opened it.

His mother said, "Oh, dear! That means *another* clean shirt!"

What do you think happened?
What should Mark have done so that wouldn't happen?

"Well," said Mrs. Breezy, "you'd better go upstairs and put on another clean shirt."

Mark said, "I don't think I have any more clean shirts."

But he found he had just one more, and he put it on.

Let's try to count how many clean shirts Mark has used this morning.

Manolita's Real Magic

Manolita liked to dress up like a magician and go around waving a magician's wand. She looked so much like a magician that some children believed she really was one—but not Ferdie.

"You can't really do magic, can you?" said Ferdie.

"Oh, yes, I can," said Manolita, although she wasn't really sure she could.

Ferdie was surprised. "You can?" he said. "I'd like to see some of your magic."

"All right," said Manolita, looking up at the cloudy sky. "I'll make it rain."

Manolita waved her wand at the sky and said, "Rain, rain, come down." But nothing happened. "This may take a while," Manolita said, and she walked through the park, waving her wand and saying over and over, "Rain, rain, come down."

Finally a few drops of rain fell. Manolita jumped up and down, shouting, "I did it! I did it! I did some real magic!"

Do you think it was real magic?
Do you think it would have rained if Manolita *hadn't* waved her wand and said, "Rain, rain, come down"?

"I don't think that was magic," said Ferdie. "It's a cloudy day. I think it was going to rain anyway."

"If you don't like that magic, I'll do something else," said Manolita. "See that bird over there on the fence? I'll make it fly away."

Manolita waved her wand and said, "Bird, bird, fly away." But the bird just sat there. Manolita moved closer to the bird, waved her wand some more, and shouted, "Bird, bird, fly away—and I mean it!" Still the bird sat there. Then Manolita moved even closer and waved her wand harder and shouted even louder. This time the bird flew away.

"I did it again!" cried Manolita, jumping up and down.

Do you think it was real magic?
Why do you think the bird flew away?

"I think you just scared that bird," said Ferdie.

Manolita's Real Magic 63

"I scared him with my magic," said Manolita. "But if you don't like that magic, I'll do something else." They were still walking in the park and had come to the top of a hill. Some child had left a wagon at the top of the hill. "See this wagon," said Manolita. "I'm going to make it move with magic."

How might Manolita make the wagon move?

Manolita waved her wand over the wagon and said, "Wagon, wagon, roll away." But the wagon just sat there. Manolita waved her wand even harder and shouted, "Wagon, wagon, this is Manolita the Magician speaking, and I'm telling you that you'd better roll away if you know what's good for you!" The wagon still sat there. Manolita, who was quite angry by this time, gave it a kick. Suddenly the wagon started to move, and it rolled all the way to the bottom of the hill.

"I did it again!" shouted Manolita, jumping up and down. "You'll have to admit that was real magic."

Do you think it was real magic?
Why do you think the wagon rolled down the hill?

"I don't think that was magic," said Ferdie. "The wagon rolled because you kicked it."

"That was part of the magic," said Manolita. "When my magic wand doesn't work, I sometimes have to use my magic foot."

Is Manolita's foot really magic?
How do you know?

Mrs. Nosho Gets Ready for a Trip

Mrs. Nosho was getting ready to go on a trip. She had to pack the clothes she would need, so she got out a suitcase and set it beside the bed. But she couldn't open it.

Why do you think she couldn't open it?

The suitcase was locked.

Mr. Nosho stopped in the doorway. "Is there anything I can do to help you get ready?" he asked.

"Yes," said Mrs. Nosho, waving her hand toward the suitcase and the rest of the room. "Please unlock it."

Does Mr. Nosho know what she wants him to unlock?

Mr. Nosho unlocked the door to the porch. "No," said Mrs. Nosho, "not that."

What do you think he'll unlock now?

He unlocked the door to the next bedroom. "No," said Mrs. Nosho. "Unlock the lock for my clothes."

What do you think he'll unlock now?

Mr. Nosho went to the closet. "The closet is already unlocked, dear," he said.

"No," said Mrs. Nosho. "For my clothes when I go away."

Does he know what she wants him to unlock now?

Finally Mr. Nosho saw the suitcase and unlocked it.

"Is there anything else I can do?" asked Mr. Nosho.

"Yes," said Mrs. Nosho. "There's something you could get for me." She was thinking of the soft little pillow from the couch. She liked to take it along on trips because sometimes the pillows in hotels were too hard. "You know, for my head."

Does Mr. Nosho know what she wants? What do you think he will bring?

66 Mrs. Nosho Gets Ready for a Trip

Mr. Nosho brought Mrs. Nosho's blue hat.

**Was that something for her head?
Was it what she wanted?**

"No," said Mrs. Nosho. "Something for my head, but for inside."

**Now does Mr. Nosho know what she wants?
What do you think he might bring next?**

Mr. Nosho brought a bottle of aspirin for headaches.

**Was that something for her head?
Was it what she wanted?**

"I don't mean for a headache," said Mrs. Nosho. "I mean to put my head on when I sleep."

Now does he know what she wants?

"Oh," said Mr. Nosho. He brought her the soft little pillow from the couch.

"Is there anything else I can get?" asked Mr. Nosho.
"Yes, I do need something else," said Mrs. Nosho. "For outdoors."

What do you think he might bring?

Mr. Nosho brought Mrs. Nosho her winter coat.
"No," said Mrs. Nosho. "Too heavy."

**Does he know exactly what she wants now?
What do you think he might bring next?**

Mr. Nosho brought her a light jacket.
"No," said Mrs. Nosho. "I'll get wet in that. They're having rainy weather out there."

Now does he know what she wants?

Mr. Nosho brought Mrs. Nosho her raincoat.
"Thank you. Now I need something for cleaning."

What do you think he might have brought?

Mr. Nosho brought Mrs. Nosho a broom.
"No," said Mrs. Nosho. "I want to clean my feet."

**Did he know exactly what she wanted then?
What might he bring next?**

Mr. Nosho brought some soap and a wash cloth.
"No, I mean I want to clean what's on my feet after I've been walking on a muddy street."

Then did he know what she wanted?

Mr. Nosho brought Mrs. Nosho a shoe brush.

"Is there anything else I can do?" he asked.
"Yes," said Mrs. Nosho. "Sit and talk to me while I do the rest of the packing myself. It will be quicker."

Did Mr. Nosho know exactly what Mrs. Nosho wanted him to do this time?

Mrs. Nosho Gets Ready for a Trip

Mr. Sleeby Tells About the Circus

When the circus came to town, Mr. Sleeby took some children to see it. When they got home, all the other children Mr. Sleeby knows came and asked him to tell about it. Mr. Sleeby always has trouble remembering the names of things he has seen, but the children don't mind. They can usually figure out what he is talking about, and it is fun for them to figure things out.

"Tell us what you saw at the circus, Mr. Sleeby," they shouted.

"Well," said Mr. Sleeby, "I saw this . . . dear me, I can't remember what it's called."

"That's O.K., Mr. Sleeby," said the children. "Tell us about everything. Tell us about the person who sold tickets, the ticket seller."

"Oh, yes!" said Mr. Sleeby. "I remember him. He walked up and down the aisles, selling us popcorn and peanuts and hot dogs and soda pop. That must have been the ticket seller."

Was that the ticket seller?
Who is Mr. Sleeby talking about?

"No!" said the children. "The person with popcorn and peanuts and soda was the *popcorn* seller. You've just got them mixed up a little."

"But that's O.K.," said the children. "Tell us about the bareback riders instead."

Mr. Sleeby went on, "Yes, the bareback riders . . . they were really exciting! They carried whips and chairs, and one of them went inside a cage with a lot of lions and made them do tricks. Those were brave riders!"

Is Mr. Sleeby talking about the bareback riders?
Who is he talking about?

One of the children said, "Mr. Sleeby, I think you're talking about the lion tamers. Bareback riders don't work with lions; they work with horses. They do tricks while riding horses."

Then another child asked Mr. Sleeby to tell them about the marching band.

"Marching band . . ." said Mr. Sleeby, "marching band . . . let me see . . . Oh, yes! They were the ones who were all dressed up and marched around . . ."

Mr. Sleeby Tells About the Circus 69

Could Mr. Sleeby be talking about the marching band?
Could he be talking about anyone else? Let's see.

"And they had paint on their faces and big, floppy shoes, and they kept doing cartwheels... I remember now."

Is Mr. Sleeby really talking about the marching band?
Who is he talking about?

"That sounds like the clowns!" said the children. "They march around like the band, but they're funny-looking, and they don't have instruments, and they do tricks."

"Oh," said Mr. Sleeby, "yes, those were the clowns."

"Gee, Mr. Sleeby, you've talked about almost everything," said one of the children, "but could you tell us just a little about the jugglers? In case you've forgotten, they're the people who throw things up in the air and catch them—real fast!"

"Jugglers?" asked Mr. Sleeby. "No, I certainly haven't forgotten about the jugglers! They were wonderful to watch, and they weren't even afraid! There they were, high up in the air, hanging by their heels from a thin little bar—then swinging back and forth. They swung from one bar, right through the air, to another bar. I thought they would fall, especially when they dove through the air and caught each other; but they didn't."

Is Mr. Sleeby talking about the jugglers?
Who is he talking about?

"Wait a minute," said Mr. Sleeby, "I remember now... I'm telling you all about the men and women on the flying trapeze! No... I don't remember the jugglers. Were they on the ground or in the air?"

Can you answer Mr. Sleeby's question?
Can you find the jugglers in the picture? [Show the illustration on page 69.]

"I wish I could remember the names better," said Mr. Sleeby, "so I could tell you about all the things I saw at the circus."

Has Mr. Sleeby told about things he saw at the circus?
Can you remember some of the things he told about?

"You *are* telling us about the things you saw at the circus," said the children. "It's all right if you don't remember the names. We like to figure things out."

Note: The objection might be raised that children shouldn't be encouraged to believe it's all right not to remember names. There's little danger that children will be encouraged by this story not to learn the names of things. On the other hand, children are sometimes hesitant to talk about their experiences for lack of key words, and they need encouragement to try.

Mark at the Bath

"Mark," said Mr. Breezy one night. "I'm not going to help you take a bath tonight."

"But I need a bath," said Mark. "Look at my arms and legs."

"You're big enough to take a bath by yourself," said Mr. Breezy. "You don't have to worry about pulling out the plug and cleaning the tub. I'll do that."

"Oh," said Mark. "How do I take a bath?"

"There are eleven things to remember," said Mr. Breezy. "You have to
put the plug in the tub,
turn on the water to fill the tub,
turn off the water when the tub is full,
put in some bath toys,
take off your clothes,
get into the tub,
scrub with soap,
rinse off with a washcloth,
get out,
use your towel, and
put on your pajamas."

So Mark went into the bathroom and took a bath by himself. He put the plug in the tub . . . turned on the water to fill the tub . . . put in some bath toys . . . took off his clothes . . . got into the tub . . . scrubbed with soap . . . rinsed off with a washcloth . . . got out . . . used his towel . . . and put on his pajamas.

Do you think he remembered everything? [If the children don't think of turning off the water, just continue the story without telling.]

"That was easy," said Mark. Then he looked at the tub and saw a lot of water running over the edge.

What had Mark forgotten to do?

"I guess I forgot to turn off the water," he said.

The next time Mark needed a bath, he asked if he could try it again by himself.

"All right," said his father. "You'll turn off the water, won't you?"

"O.K.," said Mark.

So he put the plug in the tub . . . turned on the water to fill the tub . . . turned off the water when

72　Mark at the Bath

the tub was full . . . put in some bath toys . . . took off his clothes . . . got into the tub . . . played with the toys . . . rinsed off with a washcloth . . . got out . . . used his towel . . . and put on his pajamas.

Did he remember to do everything? [If the children don't think of the soap, don't tell.]

"I'm getting pretty smart," he said. But just then he looked down at his arms and legs and saw that they were still dirty.

What had he forgotten to do?

"I guess I didn't scrub with soap." he said.

When it was time for another bath, Mark told his father that he was sure he could do it right.
"Will you remember the soap?" Mr. Breezy asked.
"Of course," said Mark. "I never make the same mistake twice."
Mark went up to the bathroom and put the plug in the tub . . . turned on the water to fill the tub . . . turned off the water when the tub was full . . . put in some bath toys . . . got into the tub . . .

Did he remember to do everything so far? [If the children don't think of Mark's taking off his clothes, don't tell.]

"I guess I forgot something," said Mark.
"Yes," said Mr. Breezy, "you were to wash yourself, not your clothes."

What had Mark forgotten to do?

"I forgot to take off my clothes," said Mark.

"Time for my bath," said Mark the next night. "I have to see if I can do it right."
"All right," said Mr. Breezy. "Go ahead."
So Mark put the plug in the tub . . . turned on the water to fill the tub . . . turned off the water when the tub was full . . . put in some bath toys . . . took off his clothes . . . got into the tub . . . scrubbed with soap . . . rinsed off with a washcloth . . . got out . . . and put on his pajamas.

Did he remember to do everything? [If the children don't think of the towel, don't tell.]

"I did it!" cried Mark. "I did it!" He ran to tell his mother and father.
"Your pajamas are all wet!" said his mother.

What had Mark forgotten to do?

"I think I forgot to use my towel," said Mark.

"I guess I'm just not big enough," said Mark sadly.
"Oh, I don't know," said Mrs. Breezy. "There are a lot of other things you could have forgotten."
"Like what?" asked Mark.
"Suppose you forgot to put the plug in the tub," said Mrs. Breezy.

What would happen?

"The tub would never get full," said Mark.

"Or suppose you forgot to get out of the tub, and you used your towel and put on your pajamas while you were still sitting in the water."

What would happen?

"My pajamas and towel would get soaking wet," said Mark.

"Or suppose you forgot to put on your pajamas at all."

What would happen?

"I'd get cold!" said Mark.

"Or suppose you forgot to put in some bath toys."

What would happen?

"Oh, I'd never forget that," said Mark. "If I forgot the bath toys, taking a bath wouldn't be any fun at all."

25

Mr. Mudanza Buys Christmas Presents

Remember Mr. Mudanza? He's the man who likes to change things. Every time he gets something new, he changes it a little.

Every Christmas Mr. Mudanza buys presents for the children he knows. But as soon as he gets the presents home from the store . . .

What do you think he does to those presents?

He changes them a little.

Last Christmas Mr. Mudanza bought Ferdie a toy horse with a saddle and rider on it. When he was getting ready to wrap the present, he said, "I'll bet Ferdie would rather have an animal that's a little wilder than a horse. I think I'll change it a little."

Now get a picture in your mind of the horse and saddle and rider.

First he threw away the rider and saddle.

Can you get a picture of that horse with no saddle and no rider?

Then he painted the horse all white.

Can you see that horse all alone and painted white?

Then he painted black stripes all over that white horse.

Can you see that—a horse painted white, with black stripes all over it?
Does it look like a horse any more?
What does it look like? (a zebra)

Mr. Mudanza bought Portia a big stuffed toy lion. Then he thought, "That's a fierce-looking animal! I think I'll change it a little and make it into an animal that looks friendlier."

Can you get a picture of that fierce-looking stuffed lion in your mind?

First Mr. Mudanza cut off the long hair at the end of the lion's tail and the hair around the lion's neck.

Can you picture how that big stuffed lion looks with no hair on its neck and its tail cut short?

Then he painted a smile on the animal's face.

Can you picture that animal with a smile on its face?
Does it look so fierce now?

Then he took some stuffing out of the lion, so it looked much smaller.

Does it look like a fierce lion any more?
What does it look like? (a house cat) [If the children say "a cat," remind them that a lion is a cat.]

Mr. Mudanza bought Mark a pair of leather snow boots. "These are nice snow boots," said Mr. Mudanza, "but I'm afraid Mark won't wear them. I think I'll change them a little bit."
First he cut the tops right off those boots!

Can you picture those boots with the tops cut off?

Then he cut an opening down the front of each boot.

Can you picture those boots with the tops cut off and an opening down the front of each boot?

Then he punched holes on each side of the openings he had made down the front.

Can you see those boots with no tops, with openings down the front, and with holes punched on each side of the openings?

And then he put laces through the holes and tied them in a bow.

Get a good picture of those boots now . . . with no tops and with openings down the front and holes on each side of the openings and laces through the holes.
Do they look like snow boots any more?
What do they look like? (shoes)

Mr. Mudanza bought Willy a wagon. But when he thought about it, he remembered that Willy already had a wagon like that.
So what do you think he said?

"Well," he said, "I'll just have to change it a little."
Get a picture of a wagon in your mind.

First he took off the handle and threw it away.

Can you picture that wagon with no handle on it?

Then he put a red box in front of the wagon and put two wheels under the box.

Can you see that wagon with no handle and with a red box with two wheels on the front?

Then he cut big square holes on each side of the box.

Can you see that? A wagon with no handle, behind a red box that is on wheels and has square holes in the sides? This is a tough one!

And then he put a seat and a steering wheel and a motor inside the box.

Wait now . . . Can you get a good picture of that wagon with no handle? Do you see a red box on the front of it? Can you picture the box on wheels and with big holes in the sides and with a seat and steering wheel and motor inside?
Does it look like a wagon any more?
What does it look like? (a truck or dump truck)

Mr. Mudanza had bought presents for all the other children he knew, but he still didn't have a present for his own daughter, Manolita. He knew just what Manolita wanted, but he couldn't find it in a store anywhere. So Mr. Mudanza started looking around the house for something he could change into what Manolita wanted. At last he found a little round wastebasket with straight

76   Mr. Mudanza Buys Christmas Presents

sides, about this high and this big around. [Show the dimensions with your hands: about 30 centimeters high and 20 centimeters in diameter.]

"This will be just what Manolita wants," said Mr. Mudanza, "if I change it a little."

First he cut a big cardboard circle and pasted it on top of the wastebasket.

Can you picture that wastebasket with a big cardboard circle on top of it?

Then he cut a round hole in the cardboard big enough for Manolita's head.

Can you picture that round wastebasket with a round piece of cardboard on it and a hole in the cardboard big enough for Manolita's head?

Then he painted the whole thing black and turned it upside down.

Does it look like a wastebasket any more?
What does it look like? (a top hat or magician's hat)
Now do you know what Manolita wanted for Christmas?

Manolita wanted a very special hat, the kind that people who do magic tricks wear. And that's just the kind Mr. Mudanza made.

Manolita's Answer Machine

Remember Manolita? She likes magic. She likes magic so much that she even dreams about it. One night she dreamed about a magic machine that could answer any question in the world. It would tell you anything you wanted to know, but only when you asked it a question. If you said something that wasn't really a question, it would just sit there and not say a word.

Manolita dreamed that she walked up to the machine and said, "O Magic Machine, how do I make you work?"

Has Manolita asked the machine a question? Will the machine answer?

"Just ask me any question, and I will answer it," said the machine.

Manolita jumped up and down shouting, "It works, it works, it really works! Now I can find out lots of things. I can even find out things about magic machines."

She turned back to the machine. "I'll bet there's only one machine like you in the whole world," she said, and she waited for the machine to answer.

Has Manolita asked the machine a question? Will the machine answer?

The machine didn't say a thing.
"Oh, oh," said Manolita. "The machine won't tell me."

How could Manolita find out what she wants to know?

"I know why the machine won't talk," said Manolita. "I didn't ask it a question."

What question could she ask to find out if she's right?

"Let's see," said Manolita. "I know. O Magic Machine, is there only one machine like you in the whole world?"

**Has Manolita asked the machine a question this time?
Will the machine answer?**

Manolita's Answer Machine

"Yes," said the machine. "I'm the only magic answer machine in the whole world."

Manolita went on talking to the machine. Sometimes she remembered to ask questions and sometimes she didn't.

"I don't think it's fair that birds can fly and I can't," said Manolita.

Has Manolita asked the machine a question? Will the machine answer?

The machine didn't say anything at all.

What question could Manolita have asked?

"Why can birds fly when I can't?" asked Manolita.

"They have wings," said the machine.

Manolita looked at the machine's buttons and wondered what they were all for.

"Say, you certainly have a lot of buttons to push," she said.

Has Manolita asked the machine a question? Will the machine answer?

The machine didn't say anything at all.

What question could Manolita have asked to find out what the buttons do?

"What do all those buttons do?" asked Manolita at last.

"Nothing," said the machine. "They're just for looks."

"Could I be a senator when I grow up?" said Manolita.

Has Manolita asked the machine a question? Will the machine answer?

"Yes," said the machine.

"I wish I didn't have to go to bed so early," said Manolita.

Has Manolita asked the machine a question? Will the machine answer?

The machine didn't say anything at all.

What question could Manolita have asked about going to bed early?

"Why do my mother and father make me go to bed so early?" asked Manolita.

"Because children need more sleep than grownups," said the machine.

"This magic machine is great," said Manolita. "It's almost too good to be true. Say, maybe I'm dreaming!"

Has Manolita asked the machine a question? Will the machine answer?

The machine didn't say anything at all.

What question could Manolita have asked?

"Oh! I mean, am I dreaming?" asked Manolita.

"Yes," said the machine, "and it's time to wake up." So Manolita woke up.

The Chicken Who Practiced to Be Queen

Note: Helping children form questions This is the first of several thinking stories in which Mrs. Nosho tells a story and Mark has to keep asking her questions to clarify the story. The children's task is to anticipate Mark's questions. This is a difficult task for many young children. They are used to answering questions but not to asking questions on demand. If the children do not catch on immediately to what is expected, it may be best to read the story through to them first without pausing for questions. Then go through the story again soon in the usual way. The children can then use memory to help them produce the appropriate questions. Although these question-asking stories may be somewhat harder than the other thinking stories, it is worth some effort to get the children to master them. Becoming an active listener—one who notices missing information and asks appropriate questions—is a very important part of a child's education.

Mrs. Nosho was telling Mark a story.

"Once upon a time," said Mrs. Nosho, "there was a chicken who wanted to be . . . who wanted to be something else."

"Pardon me," said Mark. "I have a question."

What do you think Mark is going to ask?

Mark asked, "What did the chicken want to be?"

"The chicken wanted to be queen of the world," said Mrs. Nosho. "But the chicken didn't know how to become queen, so it went to talk to someone."

"Pardon me again," said Mark. "I have another question."

What question do you think Mark will ask?

Mark asked, "Whom did the chicken go to talk to?"

"Why, it went to the queen, of course," said Mrs. Nosho. "The queen told the chicken what to do, and then the chicken went home to practice."

"Pardon me," said Mark.

82　The Chicken Who Practiced to Be Queen

What do you think Mark will ask?

Mark asked, "What did the queen tell the chicken to do?"

"The queen told the chicken to practice wearing a crown on its head. But the chicken didn't have a crown so it practiced wearing something else instead."
"Pardon me," said Mark.

What do you think Mark will ask?

Mark asked, "What did the chicken wear on its head instead of a crown?"

"It wore the glass bowl that its owner put grain in for feeding the chickens. The bowl was heavy like a crown, but the chicken had an accident because of the thing that was wrong with it."
"Pardon me," said Mark.

What do you think Mark will ask?

"What was wrong with the bowl?" Mark asked.

"The bowl came down over the chicken's eyes so it couldn't see where it was going," said Mrs. Nosho. "That's why the chicken ran into a wall and broke the bowl."
"Pardon me," said Mark. "I still don't understand. Didn't you say it was a glass bowl?"
"Yes," said Mrs. Nosho.

Why do you think Mark asked about the bowl?

"Then why couldn't the chicken see through the bowl, if it was made of glass?" asked Mark.

Why do you think the chicken couldn't see through the glass bowl?

"Because it was a very dirty bowl," said Mrs. Nosho.
"Now, when the chicken's owner found that the bowl was broken, she was very angry and said, 'No food for you today, proud bird.' Then the chicken said something, and that's the end of the story."
"Pardon me," said Mark. "I have another question."

Why is Mark asking another question? Isn't the story over?

Mark asked, "What did the chicken say?"
"The chicken said, 'Now I've learned my lesson. Next time I decide to be queen, I'm going to use a clean bowl.'"

The Chicken Who Practiced to Be Queen

Ferdie and the Big Boys

Ferdie was running very fast because he was scared! He had teased some big boys at school and they were trying to catch him. Ferdie didn't know where to hide, because the boys might already be hiding in different places, just waiting for him.

"I don't know where to hide," thought Ferdie. "I'd better try to get home as fast as I can. I can hide at home, where I know I'll be safe."

As Ferdie turned a corner, he saw a barrel lying on its side in the grass. The barrel moved a little bit as he came near it.

"Maybe I can hide in that barrel," he thought.

**What could have made that barrel move?
Is it a safe place to hide? Why or why not?
Could one of the big boys be hiding there?**

"I'd better not," Ferdie thought. Then he saw a high brick wall. He could see a policeman's hat above the wall and he wondered if he should hide from the boys behind the wall.

**Could the boys be hiding there?
Is that a safe place to hide? Why or why not?**

Ferdie kept on running until he came to a wooden fence. He looked through a hole in the fence and saw an eye staring out at him.

Is that a safe place for Ferdie to hide? Why or why not?

"I'm going to hurry home," thought Ferdie, and he kept right on running. Just then he saw a big tree that he could climb. He looked up in the tree and saw something white like a T-shirt.

**Should Ferdie hide in that tree? Why or why not?
Could one of the big boys be in that tree? Why do you think so?**

Ferdie ran a little faster. He was still a long way from home. He saw a parade coming down the street. "Say," he thought, "maybe I should join that parade and hide in it."

Ferdie and the Big Boys 85

Is it safe for Ferdie to hide in that parade? Why or why not?

Across the street was a movie theater. "Or I could go into that movie and hide there for a while," thought Ferdie.

Is the movie a safe place for Ferdie to hide? Why or why not?

"No, I can't be sure. I don't know. I'd better go on home," Ferdie thought.

He ran and ran and ran. He was almost home when he saw a big box with the lid off. There were some dogs barking at the box, but that's all Ferdie could see.

Why might the dogs be barking at that box? Is that a safe place to hide? Why or why not?

Just then Ferdie saw a woman who had spilled some groceries on the sidewalk. She looked as if she needed some help picking them up. Ferdie thought about stopping to help her, but he was afraid that the boys might get him if he did.

Would Ferdie be safe if he stopped to help the woman? Why or why not?

"Sorry I can't stop to help you," shouted Ferdie, and he hurried on. He ran around a corner and down his own street. He could see his mother calling him from the front steps of the apartment building. He ran a little faster. "Now I can hide," he thought, and he ran past his mother and into the building.

Is that a safe place for Ferdie to hide? Why or why not?

By the time he got upstairs, Ferdie was so tired he couldn't run another step. "Whew!" he said. "If I ever tease those big boys again, I'm going to do it when I'm closer to home."

Do you think that Ferdie should ever tease the big boys again? Why or why not?

86   Ferdie and the Big Boys

29

Manolita's Second Magic Machine

Do you remember Manolita's magic machine that answered questions?

Is there really a machine like that?

No, Manolita only dreamed about that machine. She often dreamed about magic. One night she dreamed about another magic machine that could do even more fantastic things than the first one. This machine could make anything in the world. You could talk into this machine, tell it what to make, and right away it would shoot out whatever you told it to make. It was like a bubble-gum machine, but much, much bigger.

There was just one little problem with the machine. If you said the name of the thing you wanted, it would not make it; but if you told the machine *about* the thing you wanted, without saying its name, the machine would make exactly what you told it to make.

In her dream, Manolita walked right up to that machine and said, "I want some roller skates!"

Did Manolita say the name of the thing she wanted?
Will that machine make it for her? Why not?

Manolita waited, but the machine didn't make anything, because she told it the *name* of the thing she wanted—roller skates.

What should Manolita tell the machine?

"Come on, you silly machine!" said Manolita. "I'm dreaming about you, and you're supposed to be magic! I want some metal things with wheels on them and straps that fit over my shoes."

This time did Manolita say the name of the thing she wanted?
Will the machine make roller skates for her?

No sooner had Manolita told the machine about what she wanted than out shot a pair of roller skates.

"Oh, good!" said Manolita. "You are magic, you really are magic!"

88 Manolita's Second Magic Machine

Manolita wanted so many things that she had to stop and think about what to say next. Most of all she wanted a toy car that she could ride in.

"Let me see," said Manolita. "I'd better be careful and not say its name. I know what to say: 'Machine, I want something that has four wheels and that I can sit in.' "

Will the machine make a toy car?
What could it make?

No sooner had Manolita told the machine what she wanted than out shot a wagon.

Did Manolita want a wagon?
Did the machine do what Manolita told it to do?
What could Manolita tell the machine so it would make a toy car and not something else?

"Oh, dear," said Manolita. "I'd better change what I said a little. Let me see . . . I want a toy that has four wheels and a steering wheel and that I can drive—and I want it to look just like the real one my dad has, only smaller."

Will the machine make a toy car this time?

No sooner had Manolita told the machine what she wanted than out shot a toy car.

"That's just what I wanted," said Manolita. "Now what do I want next?" She thought a long time. She didn't want to get just any old thing. "I know what I'd like," she thought. "I'd like a typewriter of my own, like the ones in offices."

Manolita told the machine, "I want something all my own that I can write letters with."

Did Manolita say enough?
What could the machine make her?

No sooner had Manolita told the machine what she wanted than out popped a pencil.

Did Manolita want a pencil?
Did the machine make a mistake? Why not?
What could Manolita tell the machine so it would make a typewriter?

"I don't want a pencil," said Manolita. "I already have one. I'd better change what I said a little." Then Manolita talked into the machine: "Listen, I want something that's a machine, and you write letters with it by poking on it with your fingers."

Will the machine make a typewriter this time?

No sooner had Manolita told the machine what she wanted than out shot a big, real typewriter.

"This magic machine is doing such a great job for me," said Manolita, "that I'm going to see if it will make me something no other child in the world has. I'm going to see if it will make me a real jet airplane!"

Manolita said to the machine, "I want something that flies very fast."

Could that be a jet airplane?
Could it be anything else? What?

No sooner had Manolita told the machine what she wanted than out zoomed the fastest fly that she had ever seen.

"That's not what I want," said Manolita. "I'll try again. I want something that's big and shiny and that I can fly in fast by myself."

Will the machine make a jet airplane this time?

For a minute the machine didn't do anything, and then out popped a little card with writing on it. The card said, "It sounds as if you want a real jet airplane, but you said you wanted to fly in it by yourself. There's no jet airplane in the world that someone as young as you can fly in alone. Sorry."

"Oh, well," said Manolita, "I'll have to think of something that makes a little more sense. I know something. It sounds silly, but I'd love to have a real live giraffe." So she said to the machine, "I want a big wild animal that has four legs, a long tail, and spots all over it."

Could that be a giraffe?
Could it be anything else? What?
What else should Manolita say if she wants to be sure she gets a giraffe?

Manolita's Second Magic Machine

No sooner had Manolita told the machine what she wanted than out jumped a big spotted leopard, which started growling at her. Manolita was really scared!

How do you think Manolita could have escaped from the leopard?

"I'd better do something fast," thought Manolita. She shouted into the machine, "Make me something that will wake me up right away!"

What could the machine make?

No sooner had Manolita shouted what she wanted than out popped an alarm clock, which was ringing loudly. Manolita woke up just in time to get away from that big spotted leopard. "You have to be careful what you say to that machine," said Manolita. "I'm glad I didn't make a mistake when I asked for the alarm clock!"

30

The Farmer Who Found a Giant in His Barn

Note: See story 27, "The Chicken Who Practiced to Be Queen," for suggestions on presenting this kind of story.

Mrs. Nosho was telling Mark a story about a farmer who found a giant in his barn.

"The farmer went to a wise man," said Mrs. Nosho, "to ask him how he could get that giant out of his barn.

" 'Use this,' said the wise man, and he gave the farmer something."

"Pardon me," said Mark. "I have a question."

What question do you think Mark will ask?

Mark asked, "What did the wise man give the farmer?"

"A metal bucket," said Mrs. Nosho. "Then the farmer did something odd with the bucket."

"Pardon me," said Mark. "I have another question."

What question do you think Mark will ask now?

"What did the farmer do with the bucket?" asked Mark.

"He put it over his head to scare the giant. He thought the giant would think he was a monster, and that this would make the giant run away. Well, the giant did think he was a monster, but the giant didn't run away."

"Pardon me," said Mark.

What do you think Mark will ask?

"Why didn't the giant run away?" asked Mark.

"The giant wasn't scared," said Mrs. Nosho. "The giant said, 'You're a very small monster. I'm not afraid of you.'

" 'That didn't work,' thought the farmer. 'I wish that wise man had told me how to use the bucket.' Then he thought of something else to try, and he tried it."

"Pardon me," said Mark.

What will Mark ask?

92 The Farmer Who Found a Giant in His Barn

Mark asked, "What else did he try?"

"The farmer tried putting the bucket on one foot like a shoe and walking in it, and this *did* scare the giant."
"Pardon me," said Mark.

What will Mark ask?

"Why did this scare the giant?" asked Mark.

"The giant heard a loud, slow CLANK . . . CLANK . . . CLANK . . . as the bucket hit the ground. This made him believe something that wasn't true."
"Pardon me," said Mark.

What do you think Mark will ask?

"What did the giant believe that wasn't true?" asked Mark.

"He believed that a big metal giant was coming toward the barn very slowly: CLANK . . . CLANK . . . CLANK . . . But he didn't run away. He did something else instead."
"Pardon me," said Mark.

What will Mark ask?

"What did the giant do?" asked Mark.

"He just locked the barn door so the metal giant couldn't get in," said Mrs. Nosho. "Well, the farmer was very disappointed. 'The wise man must have been wrong,' he thought. 'I don't think I'll ever be able to scare the giant away with this metal bucket. I guess I'll just have to try to make friends with the giant!' But when he went to tell the giant that he wanted to be friends with him, he couldn't tell him."
"Pardon me," said Mark.

What will Mark ask?

"Why couldn't he tell the giant he wanted to be friends?" asked Mark.

"Because the giant was asleep. The farmer shouted and shouted at him and couldn't wake him up. Finally the farmer tried something else, and it woke up the giant."
"Pardon me," said Mark.

What will Mark ask?

"How did the farmer wake up the giant?" asked Mark.

"He pounded on the metal bucket with a rock," said Mrs. Nosho. "It woke up the giant, and the giant ran away."
"Pardon me," said Mark.

What will Mark ask?

"Why did the giant run away?" asked Mark.

"When the giant heard the pounding, he thought it was the drums of an army. And he knew he couldn't fight a whole army, so he ran away.

"The farmer was puzzled, because of course he didn't know why the giant had run away.

" 'That's a strange giant,' said the farmer. 'He wasn't afraid to be my enemy, but he's afraid to be my friend.' "

31
Two of Everything

One afternoon, just after Mrs. Nosho came home from work, Ferdie and Portia went over to visit her.

"Let me show you my big dog," said Mrs. Nosho. Ferdie and Portia followed her out to the yard. There was the big dog, chained to its big doghouse.

"Growl!" growled the big dog.

"Stay away from him," said Mrs. Nosho. "He bites people if he doesn't know them."

As they walked around the yard, Mrs. Nosho said, "Watch out! Don't trip over my dog's dish." Portia looked down and saw a tiny little dish.

"That dish isn't big enough to feed that dog of yours," said Portia.

"Yes, it is," said Mrs. Nosho. "My dog is just the right size for that dish."

How could that dish be just right?
What size dog could use that dish?

Ferdie thought a minute and said, "Do you have another dog, Mrs. Nosho?"

Why did Ferdie ask Mrs. Nosho if she had another dog?

"Why, yes, Ferdie," said Mrs. Nosho, "and here it is." Just then a tiny little dog ran into the yard. "And this little dog is very, very friendly."

They walked toward the house. Portia saw a big leather thing on the ground.

"What's this thing?" she asked.

"Oh, that thing is called a muzzle. Sometimes I have to put it over my dog's nose and mouth so he doesn't bite people," said Mrs. Nosho.

"But you said it was a very friendly dog," said Portia, moving away from the little dog. "And it seems awfully big for this little dog's nose and mouth."

Was that muzzle for the little dog? Why not?
Which dog was the muzzle for?

"Portia," said Ferdie, "that's for the other dog."

How did Ferdie know it was for the other dog?

"Why do you have two dogs?" asked Portia.

"Oh, I like to have two of everything . . ." said Mrs. Nosho, "except children. Mr. Nosho and I have three children, you know. There they are, over by our car." Mr. Nosho and the children and the dogs were in front of the garage, beside a tiny car with only two seats in it.

"How can you get your three children, your two dogs, your husband and yourself into that little bitty car?" asked Portia. "And why don't you keep your car in the garage?"

Could Mrs. Nosho get herself and her family and dogs into that little car?
Why do you think her car is not in the garage?

Mrs. Nosho laughed, "I don't take my whole family and dogs in that car, Portia. That little car is the car I drive to work. We have another car in the garage. That's why I have to keep my little car outside."

What size car do you think is in the garage?

"Let's go into the house," said Mrs. Nosho. As they walked into the house, Portia saw an umbrella by the door. It was very pretty, but it was made of paper.

"Mrs. Nosho," said Portia, "I'm afraid you're going to have trouble with this umbrella. It's made of paper, and the rain will soak right through it and ruin it. If it gets too wet, it will probably tear."

Can you think of any reason why Mrs. Nosho might buy a paper umbrella?
Can you use an umbrella when it's not raining?
Could you use an umbrella when it's very hot and sunny?

"I have another umbrella for the rain," said Mrs. Nosho. "When it's very hot outside, I use this paper umbrella to shade me from the hot sun."

"That's a pretty good idea," said Ferdie. "Whenever I get too hot in the summer, I go swimming in the swimming pool. That works even better than an umbrella."

"Well," said Mrs. Nosho, "we have a swimming pool, but we only use it when it's very cold outside."

"Mrs. Nosho," said Portia, "that's really funny. Why would you swim in a swimming pool only when it's cold outside?"

Can you figure out anything about the Noshos' swimming pool?
Where do you think their pool is?

"We really like to swim all the time, Portia. So we're very lucky to have a swimming pool inside our house. That way we can swim even when it's too cold to swim outside," said Mrs. Nosho.

Just then the Noshos' children came running in from outdoors, all dripping wet in their swimming suits. "Now I'm really confused," said Portia. "Why were your children outside in their swimming suits if your swimming pool is inside?"

Can you think of a reason?
Where do you think the Noshos swim when the weather is warm?

Ferdie whispered to Portia, "Two swimming pools."

"Oh, I understand," said Portia. "You have one swimming pool inside and one swimming pool outside."

"That's right," said Mrs. Nosho. "I like to have two of everything."

"You have two dogs," said Ferdie, "and two cars and two umbrellas and two swimming pools. It must cost a lot of money to have two of everything!"

"Yes, it does," said Mrs. Nosho. "That's why I also have two jobs. Now, if you'll excuse me, it's almost nighttime and I have to leave for work."

"But you just came home from work," said Portia. "Oh, yes, I understand."

Coffee at Grandmother's House

"Mark," said Mr. Breezy, "would you call your grandmother and ask her if we can go over and see her tonight?"

"All right," said Mark, "but you'd better tell me exactly how to do it, so I don't forget anything."

"That's a good idea," said Mr. Breezy. "Here are the things you have to do: Go to the phone. Pick up the receiver. Say hello to your grandmother. Ask her if tonight is a good time to visit."

**Did Mr. Breezy leave out anything?
What will happen if Mark does exactly what he was told?** [If the children don't notice anything wrong, say "Listen again" and reread the list.]

Mark did as his father told him, but his grandmother didn't say anything to him. In fact, all he heard on the phone was a buzz.

Why did Mark hear a buzz on the phone?

"Dad," said Mark, "all I heard on the phone was a buzz."

"That's funny," said Mr. Breezy. "I must have forgotten to tell you to dial the number. You do that right after you pick up the receiver. Do you want to try again?"

Mark did, and that night he and his mother and father went to visit Grandmother.

"I'd like to make you some coffee in my new electric coffeepot," said Grandmother, "but I've never used it before and I'm not sure I know how to make coffee with it."

"That's easy," said Mr. Breezy. "I can tell you exactly what to do. First you put four cups of water in the coffeepot. Then you put in that metal thing. Then you put the lid on. Then you plug in the coffeepot and wait until the little red light goes on. Then you pour the coffee."

"Are you sure that's all I have to do?" asked Grandmother. "I know that sometimes you tell people things they don't need to do and other times you forget to tell people things they do need to do."

"I'm sure I told you exactly what to do," said Mr. Breezy.

"All right," said Grandmother. "I'll do it, but I'm not sure you'll like the coffee when I'm through."

Grandmother put four cups of water in the pot, put in the metal strainer, plugged in the pot,

Coffee at Grandmother's House

waited until the light went on, and then started to fill the coffee cups. But what came out of the pot didn't look like coffee at all. It looked just like water.

What did Mr. Breezy forget to tell Grandmother to do? (put in the coffee)

"That's not coffee; that's water," said Mark.

"I know it is," said Grandmother with a sly smile.

Mr. Breezy laughed. "I'll bet you knew that would happen, didn't you?" he said to Grandmother.

"Yes," said Grandmother. "I've learned a few things in my years, and one of them is that if you want to make coffee, you need to put coffee in the pot."

When the family got home, Mr. Breezy told Mark to do his homework and then go to bed. "Listen very carefully," said Mr. Breezy. "Go to your room. Turn on the light. Pick up your book. Think very hard. Put down your book. Turn off the light. And get into bed."

Did Mr. Breezy leave out anything?
What will happen if Mark does exactly what he was told?

Mark did as his father told him, but when he got up in the morning, he couldn't remember any of his homework. "I don't know why it is," said Mark to his father, "but I just didn't learn anything."

"That's funny," said Mr. Breezy. "I must have forgotten to tell you to read the book. Well, I'll try to remember to tell you next time!"

Mr. Sleeby's Toy Store

You're probably wondering what kind of work Mr. Sleeby does. Well, Mr. Sleeby runs a toy store. It's a good toy store. It has every kind of toy. The only trouble is that Mr. Sleeby can never remember the names of the toys.

One day Ferdie and Portia went into Mr. Sleeby's toy store to spend their birthday money.

"What can I do for you?" Mr. Sleeby asked.
"I want a ball," said Portia.
"Ball?" said Mr. Sleeby. "What's that?"

What should Portia say?

Portia said, "A ball—well, it's round."
"Oh," said Mr. Sleeby, "now I know what you want." He brought her a top.

Did Portia say enough about the ball?
What should she say to make sure she gets a ball?

"You throw it," said Portia.
"Now I know," said Mr. Sleeby, and he brought her a toy flying saucer.

What else should Portia say?

Portia said, "You bounce it."
Then Mr. Sleeby knew what Portia wanted, and he brought her a red bouncy ball.

"Would you like anything else?" Mr. Sleeby asked Portia.
"Yes, I'd like a toy train," Portia said.

What do you think Mr. Sleeby asked her next?

"Train? What's that?" Mr. Sleeby asked.
Portia was in trouble. She didn't know how to say what a train was. All she could say was, "It has wheels."

Do you think Mr. Sleeby will bring her a train?
What things could he bring her?

What Mr. Sleeby brought her was a doll buggy.
"That's not what I want," Portia said. "I want a train."

Mr. Sleeby's Toy Store 101

"You said it has wheels," said Mr. Sleeby. "See, this thing has wheels."

"Tell him more about a train," whispered Ferdie.

"I can't," whispered Portia. "All I can think of about a train is that it has wheels."

Could you say more about a train than that? What?

Poor Portia couldn't think of another thing to say, so she got down on her hands and knees and crawled around in a circle, going "Choo-choo-choo."

"Why didn't you say so?" said Mr. Sleeby. "You want one of those things that runs around on a track and goes 'Choo-choo.'" Right away he brought Portia a toy train.

"Now, what would you like, Ferdie?" Mr. Sleeby asked.

"I'd like a present for Linda Corry," said Ferdie. "I think I'll get her a marching toy soldier."

"Marching toy soldier?" said Mr. Sleeby. "What's that?"

What should Ferdie say?

Ferdie said, "Marching toy soldier—well, it moves."

Mr. Sleeby brought out the spinning top again.

Did Ferdie say enough about the toy soldier? What could he say to make sure he gets a toy soldier?

Ferdie said, "It's like a doll. You wind it in back and its arms and legs move."

"Now I think I know what you want," said Mr. Sleeby, and he brought him a marching toy soldier.

"That's a nice toy," said Ferdie, "but I've changed my mind. I think I'd rather have a soft, cuddly toy dog."

"Oh, I know what a dog is," said Mr. Sleeby, and he brought Ferdie a wooden dog with wheels on it.

Is that the kind of dog Ferdie wanted? What's wrong with it?

"That's a dog, all right," said Ferdie, "but I want one that's soft and cuddly."

"Soft? Cuddly?" said Mr. Sleeby. "What's that?"

"Now I'm stuck," thought Ferdie. "I don't know what to tell him."

Would you know what to tell Mr. Sleeby? What would you say?

Ferdie didn't know what to say, so he picked up a pillow from a doll bed and said to Mr. Sleeby, "Here, feel this. This pillow is soft and cuddly."

"Oh," said Mr. Sleeby, "you want a dog that feels nice when you hold it against your face. Why didn't you say so?" Then he brought Ferdie a toy dog that was soft and cuddly like a pillow.

As Mr. Sleeby was putting the toys into a bag, Ferdie asked, "How much money do all these things cost?"

"Money?" said Mr. Sleeby. "What's that?"

What should Ferdie say?

Ferdie said, "Money—it's that paper stuff and metal stuff you give people when you buy things."

"Oh, yes," said Mr. Sleeby, "now I remember what money is. Well, these toys will cost you exactly eleven dollars and ninety-eight cents, plus tax."

On the way home, after they had paid for the toys, Ferdie said, "I'm surprised at Mr. Sleeby. He remembers some things very well."

What does Mr. Sleeby remember very well?

102 Mr. Sleeby's Toy Store

34

The Three Bowsers

Mrs. Nosho has a big, mean dog named Bowser. She has a friendly little dog named Bowser, too. She also has a horse named Bowser. Sometimes it's hard to tell which one she's talking about.

One day Portia and Ferdie were visiting Mrs. Nosho.

"Bowser will be glad to see you," said Mrs. Nosho.

"I guess she's talking about the big dog named Bowser," Ferdie said to Portia.

Do you think Mrs. Nosho is talking about the big, mean dog named Bowser?
Why not?

"No, Ferdie," said Portia. "She can't be talking about the big dog, because the big dog is mean. He's not glad to see anyone."

"Oh, that's right," said Ferdie. "Then she must be talking about the little dog named Bowser. Little Bowser is a very friendly dog."

Could Mrs. Nosho be talking about Little Bowser?
Could she be talking about any other Bowser?

"She might mean the horse, Ferdie," said Portia. "You always bring sugar to the horse, and the horse is always very glad to see you. Let's listen and find out what else Mrs. Nosho will say."

"Yes," Mrs. Nosho went on, "Bowser really likes what you bring."

"I guess she does mean the horse," said Ferdie.

Could Mrs. Nosho be talking about the horse?
Are you sure that Mrs. Nosho couldn't be talking about Little Bowser?
Do you know whether Ferdie brings anything to Little Bowser?

"She might mean Little Bowser, Ferdie," said Portia. "You always bring Little Bowser dog biscuits."

"Bowser certainly does like to run with you," said Mrs. Nosho.

"She means the horse," said Ferdie. "Horses like to run."

Are you sure that Mrs. Nosho is talking about the horse?
Do dogs like to run?

103

"Little Bowser likes to race you," said Portia. "I still don't know which one she means."

"Would you like to ride him?" asked Mrs. Nosho.

Now do you know whether Mrs. Nosho is talking about the horse or the little dog?
How do you know?

So Ferdie and Portia each took a ride on Bowser the horse.

After their ride, Portia asked, "Where are the dogs today?"

"Out in the doghouse," said Mrs. Nosho. "Bowser's been barking a lot lately, so we've kept him out of the house."

"Which dog do you think she's talking about now?" asked Ferdie.

"I don't know," said Portia. "They both bark a lot."

"And he hasn't been eating much," Mrs. Nosho went on. "I'm a little worried about him."

"Now I know which dog she means," said Ferdie. "She means Little Bowser. Big Bowser eats a lot."

Could Mrs. Nosho be talking about Little Bowser?
Could she be talking about Big Bowser?
Why is Mrs. Nosho worried about the dog that's not eating much?

"Mrs. Nosho said she was worried about the dog," said Portia. "Maybe it's Big Bowser, and he's sick, and that's why he's not eating much."

"Bowser's not very happy these days," said Mrs. Nosho, "but I know he'd never bite me."

"It must be Little Bowser," said Ferdie. "Little Bowser never bites."

Are you sure Mrs. Nosho is talking about Little Bowser?
Did Mrs. Nosho say that the dog she's talking about never bites?
What did she say?

"Mrs. Nosho only said the dog would never bite *her,* Ferdie," said Portia. "She's the owner. I don't think that even mean Big Bowser would bite his owner. I still don't know which dog she means."

"I haven't seen Bowser all day," said Mrs. Nosho. "Let's go find him. He'll probably be so glad to see me that he'll put his paws on my shoulders and knock me over."

Now do you know which dog Mrs. Nosho is talking about?
How do you know?

"Oh, you mean Big Bowser," said Ferdie. "I knew it all the time."

They started to walk to the doghouse.

"Mrs. Nosho," said Portia, "I think it would be easier to tell which pet you're talking about if you gave your pets different names."

"Well," said Mrs. Nosho, "other people have told me the same thing. But Bowser's a good name, and *I* always know which one I'm talking about."

35

Loretta Delivers the Valentines

Ferdie was looking out the window. "You'd better hurry with those valentines, Portia," he said. "Here comes the new letter carrier!"

Portia printed as fast as she could. Then she and Ferdie ran downstairs just as the new letter carrier was coming up to the door of their apartment building.

"Hello," Portia said. "Would you please deliver these valentines for me? I have to go now, or I'll be late for school."

The new letter carrier, whose name was Loretta, looked at the valentines. "Who are these for?" she asked.

What do you think Portia forgot to put on the valentines?

"They're for some very nice people," said Portia, and away she ran to catch up with Ferdie.

Loretta scratched her head. "No envelopes, no names, no addresses, no stamps—this is a pretty tough job for my first day. But I'll do my best."

Why did Loretta think it would be hard to deliver the valentines?

Loretta decided to read the valentines to see if she could figure out who they were for. The first one said, "Happy Valentine Day from Portia. In case you don't remember who I am, I'm Ferdie's sister."

"This valentine must be for someone who forgets things," said Loretta.

Do you know anyone in these stories who forgets things?
What things does Mr. Sleeby forget?

The second valentine said, "Happy Valentine Day to you and to Bowser and Bowser and Bowser, from Portia."

"Now that must be a strange person," said Loretta. "Someone with three somethings called Bowser! It would be hard to know what someone like that was talking about."

Do you know someone in these stories who has three Bowsers?
Is it sometimes hard to know what Mrs. Nosho is talking about?

106

Loretta Delivers the Valentines 107

The third valentine said, "Happy Valentine Day from Portia. I tried to do exactly what you told me. I bought the valentines. I wrote messages on them. I changed my socks. And I put the valentines in the mail. Did I forget anything?"

"H'm," said Loretta, "this sounds like someone who is always telling people what to do, and some of the things he or she tells them are pretty silly."

Do you know someone in these stories who is always telling people what to do?
Are some of the things Mr. Breezy tells people to do silly?

The fourth valentine said, "Happy Valentine Day from Portia. I hope you like this valentine, but it's all right with me if you change it a little."

"I guess this one is for someone who is always changing things," said Loretta. "I ought to be able to find that person."

Who, in these stories, is always changing things? (Mr. Mudanza)

The last valentine said, "Happy Valentine Day! I'm glad you're coming to my house every day. I hope we'll be friends. Portia."

"This is a hard one," said Loretta. "I don't know who comes here every day."

Do you know someone who would be coming to Portia's house every day?
Think of who it could be.

Loretta put the valentines in her bag and went off to deliver the mail. The first house she came to was Mr. Sleeby's. "Do you know anyone around here who forgets things?" she asked Mr. Sleeby.

"H'm," said Mr. Sleeby. "I can't remember."

Loretta looked happy. "Mr. Sleeby," she said, "I think I have a valentine for you."

Which valentine do you think Loretta will give Mr. Sleeby?

Loretta handed him the valentine that said, "Happy Valentine Day from Portia. In case you don't remember who I am, I'm Ferdie's sister."

Why did Loretta think that valentine was for Mr. Sleeby?

Mr. Sleeby was very pleased. "Wasn't that nice of What's-Her-Name," he said. "I'll have to remember to send her a valentine next week."

Loretta went away whistling. "That valentine was for Mr. Sleeby, all right," she thought.

Loretta kept walking until she came to a house with two mailboxes. Both boxes said "Nosho." Loretta was trying to figure out which box to put Mrs. Nosho's letters in when Mrs. Nosho came out of the house.

"Do two families live here?" asked Loretta.

"No," said Mrs. Nosho. "I have this first mailbox for letters that come from someplace and this other box for letters that come from someplace else. I like to have two of everything."

Now does Loretta know which box to put Mrs. Nosho's letters in?

"Mrs. Nosho," said Loretta, "I think I have a valentine for you."

Which valentine do you think Loretta will give her?

Loretta handed Mrs. Nosho the valentine that said, "Happy Valentine Day to you and to Bowser and Bowser and Bowser, from Portia."

Why did Loretta think that valentine was for Mrs. Nosho?

"It's a beautiful card," said Mrs. Nosho. "That reminds me. I have to go someplace. I have to send something to someone myself."

Loretta went on down the street. "Only three valentines left," she thought.

She came to Mr. Breezy's house.

"I'm very glad to have you as our new letter carrier," said Mr. Breezy. "I'll tell you how to put mail in our mailbox: You lift up the lid. You take the letters out of your bag. You tap your foot three times. You put the letters in the box. And you close the lid."

"Thanks for telling me," said Loretta. "By the way, Mr. Breezy, I think I have a valentine for you."

Which valentine do you think Loretta will give Mr. Breezy?

Loretta handed him the valentine that said, "Happy Valentine Day from Portia. I tried to do exactly what you told me. I bought the valentines. I wrote messages on them. I changed my socks. And I put the valentines in the mail. Did I forget anything?"

Why did Loretta think that valentine was for Mr. Breezy?

"Portia didn't forget a thing," said Mr. Breezy happily.

Loretta was holding the two valentines she had left when she walked up to the Mudanzas' house. "Those are pretty valentines," said Mr. Mudanza. "Would you mind if I changed them a little?"

"You can change one of them," said Loretta, "because I think it's for you."

**How did Loretta know that one of the valentines was for Mr. Mudanza?
Which one was it?**

Loretta handed him the valentine that said, "Happy Valentine Day from Portia. I hope you like this valentine, but it's all right with me if you change it a little."

"I'm happy to get such a beautiful valentine," said Mr. Mudanza. "And I'm even happier because I can change it a little."

He took off the red heart with the lace around it.

Can you picture that valentine with no red heart and no lace?

Then he drew a birthday cake, with candles, on it.

Can you picture that valentine with no red heart and no lace and with a birthday cake and candles on it?

**Does it look like a valentine any more?
What does it look like?**

"Now I have a birthday card to send to Portia on her next birthday," said Mr. Mudanza.

Loretta had only one valentine left, the one that said, "Happy Valentine Day. I'm glad you're coming to my house every day. I hope we'll be friends. Portia." She went to all the houses on her route, but she didn't find anyone to give the valentine to. After school was out, she went back to Portia's house and told her, "I delivered four of your valentines, but I never could find the person who comes to your house every day."

What do you think Portia told Loretta?

"Why, that's you," said Portia, "and I hope we *will* be friends."

A big smile crossed Loretta's face as she put the valentine in her pocket. "My friends call me Loretta," she said.

36

What's Your Trouble, Mr. Sleeby?

Most of the time Mr. Sleeby doesn't even notice that things are broken in his house. But sometimes so many things go wrong that even Mr. Sleeby begins to be bothered.

One day when Loretta the Letter Carrier came to deliver the mail, she noticed that Mr. Sleeby looked unhappy. "What's your trouble, Mr. Sleeby?" she asked.

"Lots of things," said Mr. Sleeby. "For one thing, I have a sore hand."

"How did that happen?" Loretta asked.

"It's this knife of mine," said Mr. Sleeby. "Every time I use it, I cut myself. Do you have any idea what could be wrong?"

"I don't know," said Loretta. "I'd have to see the knife."

Do you have to see the knife?
Do you have any idea what could be wrong with it?

When Loretta saw the knife, she said, "I think I see why you keep cutting yourself, Mr. Sleeby. A knife should have a handle, so you can hold it by the handle and not cut yourself."

"Oh, so that's what's wrong! No handle. I'll have to remember to fix that," said Mr. Sleeby.

How could Mr. Sleeby fix the knife?
Do you think Mr. Sleeby will remember to fix it?

"Say, you're pretty smart to figure that out," said Mr. Sleeby. "Maybe you can help me with another one of my problems. I always seem to be late getting places. I never know what time it is, even though I have this fine clock that I remember to wind every night. I know it's working because I can hear it tick; but when I look at the numbers, I just can't tell what time it is. Do you have any idea what's wrong?"

"I don't know," said Loretta. "I'd have to see the clock to know for sure."

Do you have to see the clock?
What do you think is wrong with it?

Mr. Sleeby brought Loretta the clock, and it really was ticking very loudly.

When Loretta saw the clock, she said, "I think I see why you can't tell time from that clock, Mr.

What's Your Trouble, Mr. Sleeby? 111

Sleeby. It doesn't have any hands. A clock like this one has to have hands to point to the numbers, so you can tell what time it is."

"Oh, so that's what's wrong! No hands. I'll have to fix that," Mr. Sleeby said.

Do you think Mr. Sleeby will fix the clock? How could he fix it?

"I have another problem that's much worse," said Mr. Sleeby. "I'm hungry all the time. I don't seem to be getting enough to eat."

"What's your trouble, Mr. Sleeby?" asked Loretta. "Don't you have enough food in the house?"

"Oh, I have plenty of food," said Mr. Sleeby. "But every time I fix a meal and put it on the table, the plates and cups slide off to the floor. Do you have any idea what could be wrong?"

"I don't know," said Loretta. "I'd like to have a look at your table."

Do you have to see the table?

When Loretta saw the table, she said, "I think I know why you have trouble eating at your table, Mr. Sleeby. One leg is broken off, and the table tips to one side. That's why everything slides off."

"Oh, so that's what's wrong!" said Mr. Sleeby. "A broken table leg. I'll have to remember to fix that."

Do you think Mr. Sleeby will remember to fix the table leg?

"I have one more problem," said Mr. Sleeby. "My eyes hurt a lot, but they only hurt when I try to read by the lamp in the living room. The light seems awfully bright. Do you have any idea what's wrong?"

"I can't be sure unless I see the lamp," said Loretta.

Do you have to see the lamp?
Do you remember what is wrong with it?

Mr. Sleeby took Loretta into his living room and showed her the lamp.

Loretta looked at the lamp and said, "I think I see why your eyes hurt. That lamp needs a lampshade. If it had a lampshade, the light wouldn't be so bright and it wouldn't hurt your eyes."

"Oh," said Mr. Sleeby, "I thought I fixed that once before, but I guess not. I'll have to remember to fix it."

Do you remember what Mr. Sleeby did the last time the light hurt his eyes?
Did he fix the lamp?
Where did he leave the lampshade? (behind the couch)

"Thanks very much for helping me," said Mr. Sleeby. "I'm sure things will be much better now."

Do you think that things were much better for Mr. Sleeby after that?

"I hope so," said Loretta, as she picked up her mailbag and went on her way.

After Loretta was gone, Mr. Sleeby went back into his kitchen and fixed himself a cup of coffee. He put the cup on his kitchen table, and it slid down the table onto the floor and spilled. "I wonder why every time I put something on that table it slides onto the floor," said Mr. Sleeby. "I forgot all about that when Loretta was here. I should have asked her to help me figure it out. She's pretty smart."

Why did Mr. Sleeby's cup slide down onto the floor?
Did Mr. Sleeby forget to ask Loretta about his table?
What has Mr. Sleeby forgotten?
Do you think he will fix that table?
Do you think he'll fix anything else? Why not?

112   What's Your Trouble, Mr. Sleeby?

Willy Keeps On Wishing

Willy the Wisher was all alone one day. A new boy had just moved in next door and was playing all alone in his own backyard.

"I wish I could play with him," Willy kept thinking.

Will wishing make it happen?
How could Willy make it happen?

"I see you're not playing with anyone, Willy," said his grandmother. "Would you like to go shopping with me?"

They went from store to store, and Willy's grandmother kept buying things. Soon she had so many packages that it was hard for her to hold on to all of them. Packages kept slipping out of her arms and falling to the ground. Willy would pick them up and put them back on top of the other packages in her arms.

"I wish Grandmother didn't have to carry so many packages," he thought.

Will wishing help?
What could Willy do that would help?

When they got home, the new boy wasn't in his yard any more. Willy wished that he was.

Willy's father said, "Willy, let's go to the park and kick the football around. I know how much you like that."

"I wish I didn't have to go," thought Willy, "because I have a sore toe."

What will happen to Willy's sore toe when he kicks the football?
What could Willy do to keep from having to kick the football?

Willy didn't have much fun kicking the football, because of his sore toe, but he did the best he could. When they got home, Willy looked around for the new boy and saw that he was in his own backyard again.

"I still wish I could play with him," thought Willy.

Just then he heard someone crying. It was the little boy who lived three doors away. Willy walked down to see what was the matter.

"I lost my wagon," said the little boy.

113

"That's too bad," said Willy. "I wish you had your wagon back."

What could Willy do to help the little boy get his wagon back?

Willy patted the little boy on the head, but he kept on crying. Willy started to walk home. He saw the wagon under a bush.

"I wish that wagon wasn't so far under the bush," thought Willy. "That little boy will never see it."

Will wishing make the wagon easier to see? What could Willy do?

When Willy got home, Loretta the Letter Carrier was just putting some letters into his mailbox and the new boy next door was just looking over the fence.

"What are you wishing for today, Willy?" asked Loretta.

"I'm wishing I could play with the new boy next door," said Willy.

"I just talked to him," said Loretta, "and he said he wished he could play with you. I'll take you over to meet him."

"Oh, boy," thought Willy. "I wish I knew more people like Loretta."

Willy Keeps On Wishing

Mr. Sleeby Buys New Furniture

Sometimes things get so bad at Mr. Sleeby's house—so many things are broken or lost—that the only thing left for Mr. Sleeby to do is to go out and buy new things. But it's very hard for him to remember the new things he needs, because he can never remember what's broken.

The last time Mr. Sleeby needed new furniture he had a bright idea. "I'll call that furniture store from here," he thought. "That way, I can just look around and tell the furniture store to send over the things I need—and I won't have time to forget." The only trouble was that Mr. Sleeby couldn't find his telephone anywhere. He looked and looked and then said, "Oh, well, I guess I'll have to go to that furniture store after all."

When Mr. Sleeby got to the furniture store he walked right up to the clerk and said, "I need a new . . . uh . . . well, I just can't think of the name of it. It's a lot like a chair, but it's longer than a chair."

Can you think of the name of it? (a couch)

"Oh," said the clerk, "you want a couch. The couches are over here."

Mr. Sleeby sat on one of the couches. "I'll take this one," he said. "It's nice and soft. My old couch is too hard."

Why is Mr. Sleeby's old couch too hard? (no cushions on it)

"And I need a new . . . h'm . . . well, I forget the name of it, but it looks like a stool . . . yes, it looks like a stool with a back on it."

What is Mr. Sleeby thinking of? (a chair)

"You must mean a chair. We have lots of chairs over here," said the clerk.

Mr. Sleeby sat down and leaned back in a chair.

"I like this one," he said, "and do you have a . . . well, I can tell you what it's like; it's like a desk, but it doesn't have any drawers, and I eat my meals on it."

What does Mr. Sleeby want this time? (a table)

116

Mr. Sleeby Buys New Furniture

"A table?" asked the clerk.

"That's what I want," said Mr. Sleeby.

The clerk led Mr. Sleeby to the kitchen tables. Mr. Sleeby ran his hand over the top of one of the tables.

"This table is fine," said Mr. Sleeby. "I'm sure my dishes won't slide off this one the way they do off my old table."

Do you remember what is wrong with Mr. Sleeby's old kitchen table? (A leg is broken.)

"Now, I just need a few more things," Mr. Sleeby said. "I especially need a . . . oh, my . . . it's like a couch, but it's bigger."

"I don't know of anything like that. You bought the biggest couch I have. Can't you remember the name?" asked the clerk.

Can you think of the name?

"No, but it doesn't have a back," said Mr. Sleeby, "and it has just one big cushion that you put sheets on."

Now do you know what Mr. Sleeby is talking about? (a bed)

"You must mean a bed," said the clerk. "Here they are, the very best beds in town."

"I'll take that bed," said Mr. Sleeby. "And I just need one more thing that I can remember. I need a . . . oh, dear . . . I can't remember."

"What's it like?" asked the clerk.

"It's a little bit like an alarm clock," said Mr. Sleeby, "because it's plugged into the wall, and it rings, and it has numbers on it."

Do you know what Mr. Sleeby is talking about?

"I still don't know what you want," said the clerk. "Tell me how it's different from a clock."

Mr. Sleeby thought a minute. "I can't tell time on it, and it has a different shape from a clock, and it doesn't tick, and I talk to people on it."

Do you know what Mr. Sleeby is talking about now? (a telephone)

"Oh," said the clerk, "you need a new telephone! We don't sell those here. I can't help you with that, but call the telephone company when you get home and they'll see that you get one."

Will Mr. Sleeby be able to call the telephone company when he gets home?
Why not?

When Mr. Sleeby got home he went to look again for the telephone, but he still didn't see it. Then he tripped on a cord and yanked the telephone out of the drawer where he had put it. Mr. Sleeby fell to the floor and the telephone landed on top of him. "Good," said Mr. Sleeby. "It didn't break. Now I can call the telephone company and get a new phone."

Does Mr. Sleeby need a new telephone?

39

The New Neighbors

"Come look out the window, Ferdie," called Portia. "There's a new family moving into our building."

How do you think Portia knew there was a new family moving into their building?

Ferdie ran to the window and looked out. Parked in front of their apartment building was a moving van loaded with furniture and boxes, and some men were carrying furniture from it.

"I wonder if they have children our age," Ferdie said.

How could Portia and Ferdie tell if the new family had children their age?

"Let's watch what the men bring in and see if we can tell," said Portia.

The first thing they saw the men bring in was a television set.

"They do have children our age," said Ferdie happily.

"How can you tell?" asked Portia.

"Because they have a television set just like ours. You and I watch television, so they must have children who watch television too."

Was that a good guess?
Are children the only people who watch television?

"They could be just grownups," said Portia. "Grownups watch television too."

The next thing the men brought in was a playpen. "Oh, too bad," said Ferdie, "all they have is a baby."

What made Ferdie think they had a baby?
Was it a good guess to think they had only a baby?

"They could have a baby and other children too," said Portia.

119

120 **The New Neighbors**

Then the men brought in a lot of boxes. "Now I know they have children our age," said Ferdie. "Those boxes must be filled with toys; and with all those toys, there must be a lot of children."

Was that a good guess?
Could the boxes be filled with toys?
What else could the boxes have in them?

"Maybe the boxes are full of things that belong to grownups," said Portia.

Next the men brought in two highchairs. "That baby must eat a lot if it needs two highchairs," said Ferdie.

Was that a good guess?
Can you think of any other reasons why a family might have two highchairs?

"I don't see how a baby could use two highchairs at once," said Portia.

Just then a woman came up the street, pushing a stroller with two babies in it. She stopped to talk to the moving men, and then she went inside the apartment building.

Now do you know why the family has two highchairs?
Do you think that the family could have had children that were Ferdie and Portia's ages?
Did Portia and Ferdie know yet whether the family had any children who were their ages? Why or why not?

The New Neighbors

40

Mark the Builder

Mark, Willy, and Manolita were looking at a big wagon in a toy-store window. "I wish I had that wagon," said Willy.

"If I knew the right magic, I could turn my little wagon into a big wagon like that," said Manolita.

Mark said, "Wishing won't do it. Magic won't do it. But I think I could build it."

Mark looked carefully at the wagon. Then he went home and started to build. First he found a box.

Why did he get a box?

Then he put the box out on the sidewalk and showed it to Willy and Manolita.

"See my new wagon?" he said.

Mark's friends giggled.

"What's so funny?" asked Mark. "You can sit in a wagon and ride. I can sit in my wagon and ride."

Can Mark *sit* in his wagon?
Can Mark *ride* in his wagon?

"You can't ride in that wagon," said Willy. "I wish you could, but you can't."

"Oh," said Mark, and he brought out four little wheels and put them under the wagon. "Now look at my wagon," he said. "Now I can sit in my wagon and ride. Will you pull me in my wagon, Manolita?"

Manolita giggled.

"What's so funny?" asked Mark.

"I can't pull you in that wagon," said Manolita. "Let me change it a little bit for you. Then you'll have a nice wagon."

How do you think Manolita will change the wagon?

Manolita got a long handle and stuck it on the front of the wagon.

"There," she said, "now you can sit and I can take you for a ride."

It was a windy day and many children were out flying kites. "Too bad we don't have a kite," said Manolita. "With magic we could make it fly higher than all the others."

"I'm wishing for a kite," said Willy.

"I'm thinking," said Mark. "If we got some

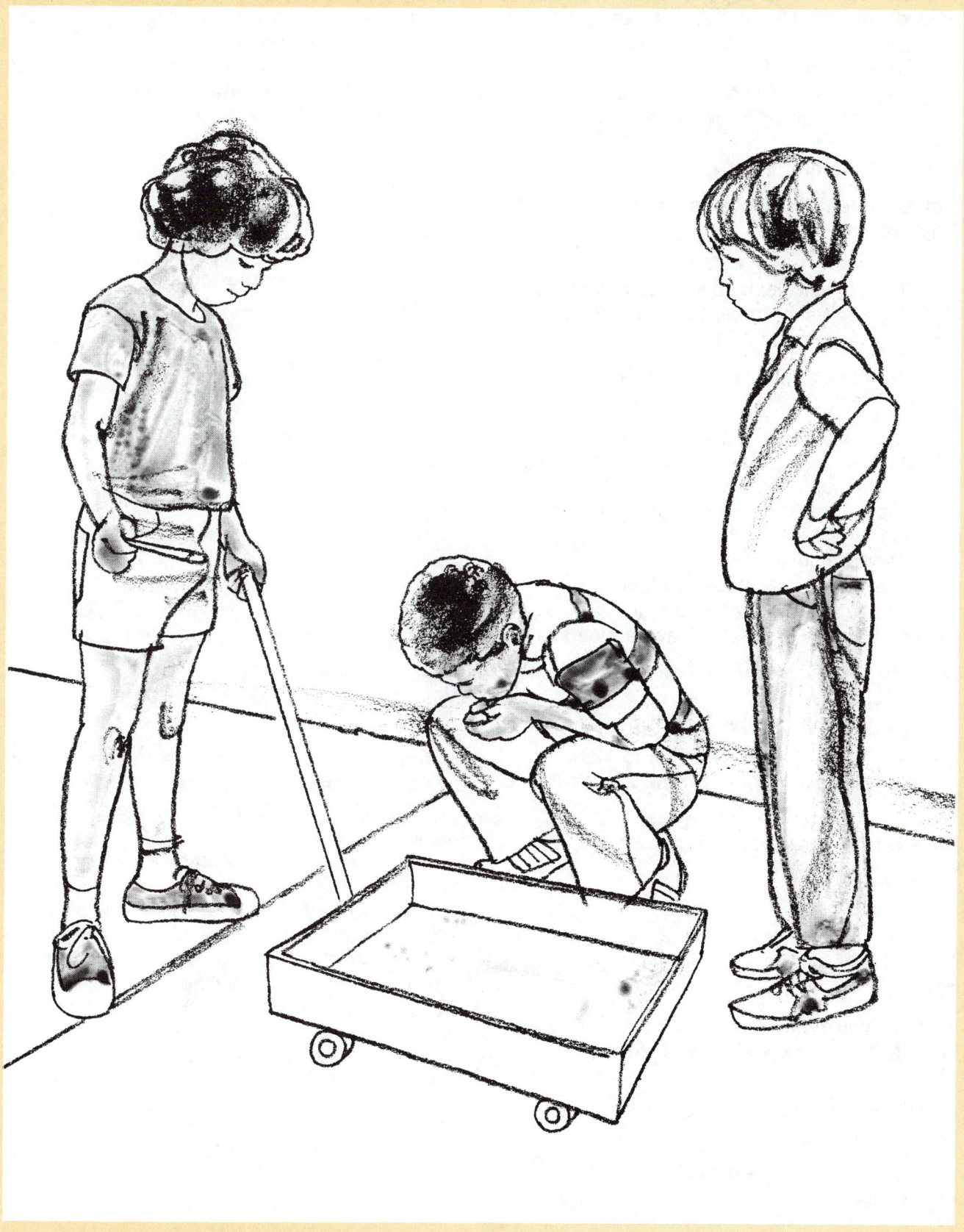

Mark the Builder 123

paper, I think I could build us a kite."

Mark found some paper and started to build. First he cut a big diamond out of paper and tied a tail on it. Then he showed it to his friends and said, "See our new kite?"

Mark's friends giggled.

"What's so funny?" asked Mark. "Willy, help me lean this kite up against the wall. Then we'll take it outside and fly it."

Can Mark lean that kite up against the wall? Why not?

"That kite can't lean up against the wall," said Willy. "It won't stay there. I wish it could, but it can't."

Do you know what's wrong with Mark's kite?

"Oh," said Mark, and he brought out some pieces of wood to make a frame for the kite. "There," he said, "now look at our kite. We can lean it up against the wall and we can take it outside and fly it."

Manolita giggled.

"What's so funny?" asked Mark.

"We can't fly that kite," said Manolita. "Let me change it a little. Then we'll have a nice kite."

What do you think Manolita will do to the kite?

Manolita got a lot of string and tied it to the kite. Then she handed the string to Mark.

"There," said Manolita, "now we can fly the kite."

**Does it take magic to fly a kite?
What does it take?**

Mark, Willy, and Manolita wanted to go fishing. "I wish I had a fishing pole," said one of them.

**Who do you think said that?
Why do you think so?**

"If I knew the right magic, I could catch fish without a fishing pole," said someone.

**Who do you think said that?
Why do you think so?**

"Wishing won't do it. Magic won't do it. But I think I could make us a fishing pole," said Mark.

First Mark found a long branch lying on the ground and broke off all the twigs so that it was just one long stick. He showed it to Willy and Manolita and said, "Now we have a fishing pole. Let's go fishing."

Mark's friends giggled.

"What's so funny?" asked Mark.

"We can use that stick for a fishing pole," said Willy, "but we won't catch any fish with it. I wish we could, but we can't."

Why won't they be able to catch fish with just that pole?

"Oh," said Mark, "I see that we need a string and something to put the worm on." So he tied one end of a string to the pole, and he tied the other end of the string to a straight pin. "There," he said, "now we can put a worm on the pin and catch a fish."

Manolita giggled.

"Now what's so funny?" asked Mark.

"Well," said Manolita, "if you put a worm on that pin, it will slide right off; and even if a fish bites it, the fish will get away. Let me change it for you a little. Then you'll have a fishhook."

**What is wrong with the pin?
What do you think Manolita will do to it?**

Manolita took a pair of pliers and bent the pin until it was shaped like a letter J.

"There," she said, "now we have a hook that might catch a fish."

You may be wondering how three children can fish with just one fishing pole. Here is how they did it. Willy sat there, wishing they would catch a fish. Manolita waved her magician's wand and said, "Fish, fish, bite our hook." And Mark put a worm on the hook and held the pole out over the water. In this way they finally caught a tiny fish, which made them very proud.

"I think we did it," said Willy, "by wishing."

"I think we did it," said Manolita, "by magic."

"I think the worm did it," said Mark, "by wriggling."

Willy's Lost Kitten

Willy the Wisher had a gray kitten that he played with every day, but one day Willy couldn't find the kitten. He stood out in his front yard, wishing. "I wish that kitten would come running to play with me," he thought.

Do you think the kitten will come running if Willy just stands there, wishing?
What should Willy do?

Willy started walking along the sidewalk, wishing he would see his gray kitten. He passed many of his friends. "Hi, Willy," they said.

"Hi," Willy said. He wished he knew whether they had seen his gray kitten.

How could Willy find out if they had seen his gray kitten?
What question should he ask?

Willy walked for a long time, and he started to get hungry. "I wish I knew what time it is," he thought. "I wish I knew if it is time to go home for lunch."

How could Willy find out what time it is?
How could he find out, if there are no clocks in sight?

Willy got hungrier and hungrier. Some children came past, eating ice-cream bars. "I wish I knew where an ice-cream store is," thought Willy. "I have a quarter and I could buy one of those ice-cream bars."

Will Willy find out where an ice-cream store is just by wishing?
What question should he ask?

Willy was starting to get very thirsty, too. He wandered past a drinking fountain. Some children were playing at the fountain, spraying water around. Willy stood there, wishing they would stop playing for a minute so he could get a drink of water.

What should Willy say to the children?

126 Willy's Lost Kitten

Finally Willy decided to go home. He walked and walked, but he couldn't find his house. He couldn't find Elm Street, where he lived. He didn't see any place he knew. "Now I'm lost too," Willy said to himself. "My kitten's lost, I'm lost, and I'm hungry and thirsty. I wish I could find my way home!"

Just then a friendly police officer came by. "How are you, young fellow?" she said.

"Fine," Willy said.

Was that a good thing for Willy to say? Why not?

What should Willy have said to the police officer so that she could help him?

"I wish that police officer had asked me what is wrong," Willy thought, "but she didn't."

Willy was standing on the sidewalk, still wishing he could get home, when Loretta the Letter Carrier came along. "Hello, Willy," she said. "You look as if you're wishing for something."

"I am," said Willy. "I'm wishing I could find my way home."

"Then walk along with me," said Loretta. "I happen to be going to your house."

Do you think that Willy's wish had come true?

Willy was surprised to hear that, but he didn't say anything. He walked along with Loretta.

Finally Loretta said, "I'll bet you wish you knew why I'm going to your house, don't you?"

"Yes," said Willy.

"Then why don't you ask me?"

"Why are you going to my house?" Willy asked.

Why might Loretta have been going to Willy's house?

"To take back something that I found on the street," said Loretta. "I have it right here in my mailbag."

Willy started to wish that he knew what Loretta had in her mailbag, but then he had an idea. He decided to ask a question.

What question would you ask if you were Willy?

Willy asked, "What do you have in your mailbag?"

What do you think Loretta might have had in her mailbag?

"I'll show you," said Loretta. She opened the mailbag, and there was Willy's gray kitten, curled up, asleep.

"I'm glad I asked what is in the mailbag," said Willy. "Now I can stop wishing. I've been doing so much wishing today that I'm getting tired."

Willy's Lost Kitten 127

Mr. Mudanza Changes Things for Mr. Sleeby

Remember Mr. Mudanza? He's the man who always likes to change everything a little.

And remember Mr. Sleeby? He's the man who forgets so many things.

Mr. Sleeby bought new furniture, if you remember, but before long it was in just as bad shape as his old furniture had been. So Mr. Sleeby asked Mr. Mudanza to come over and fix things. Mr. Sleeby showed Mr. Mudanza his kitchen table, which had a broken leg. "Do you think you can fix this?" he asked.

"Yes, I can fix it," said Mr. Mudanza, "but do you mind if I change it a little?"

"Not at all," said Mr. Sleeby. "Go ahead."

Get a picture of that kitchen table in your mind. [Show the illustration on page 111.]

First Mr. Mudanza took off all the legs.

Can you picture that table with no legs at all?

Next he stood it up on one end.

Can you see how that table would look standing up on end with the legs cut off?

Finally he put some hinges on one side of the table and a knob on the tabletop.

Can you picture that table with no legs and with some hinges on one side and a knob on top?
Does it look like a kitchen table any more?
What does it look like? (a door)

"Why, you've changed my kitchen table into a door," said Mr. Sleeby. "Say, I needed a door."

"Yes, I noticed that the door between your kitchen and living room was missing, and I thought you might like to have one," said Mr. Mudanza. "Is there anything else that needs fixing?"

"Yes," said Mr. Sleeby. "Come into my living room and let me show you my couch." The couch had two broken arms.

"I can fix your couch, Mr. Sleeby," said Mr. Mudanza, "but do you mind if I change it a little?"

"Not at all," said Mr. Sleeby.

Get a picture of that couch in your mind.

Mr. Mudanza Changes Things for Mr. Sleeby 129

First Mr. Mudanza took off the broken arms.

Can you picture that couch with no arms?

Then he took off the back.

Can you picture that couch with no arms and no back?

Finally he put a pillow and some sheets and a blanket on it.

Can you picture that couch with no arms and no back and with a pillow, some sheets, and a blanket on it?
Does it look like a couch any more?
What does it look like? (a bed)

"Oh, my!" said Mr. Sleeby. "You've changed my couch into a bed. I needed a bed because my old one is broken."

"Say, while we're here, let me show you my coat," said Mr. Sleeby. "It needs fixing too." Mr. Sleeby showed Mr. Mudanza his overcoat. The coat certainly was not handsome! The bottom of it was badly torn, and its thick lining was full of holes.
"Do you mind if I change it a little bit?" asked Mr. Mudanza.
"Go ahead," said Mr. Sleeby.

Can you get a picture of Mr. Sleeby's overcoat in your mind?

First Mr. Mundanza took out the thick lining full of holes and threw it away.

Can you picture Mr. Sleeby's overcoat without that lining?

Then he put a new thin lining in it.

Can you picture Mr. Sleeby's overcoat with a new thin lining in it?

Finally Mr. Mudanza cut off some of the overcoat and put a hem in it, so that when Mr. Sleeby put it on, the bottom of the coat came just below his middle.

Can you picture Mr. Sleeby's coat, with a new thin lining, cut just below his middle?
What does it look like? (a jacket)

"Oh," said Mr. Sleeby, "you've changed my coat into a jacket. Good! I don't think I have a jacket."
"Well," said Mr. Mudanza, "it's not cold outside and you needed something to wear that's not so warm."

"Thanks," said Mr. Sleeby. "Say, I also have a bookcase that is broken."
The bookcase had three broken shelves. Books were lying all over the floor, and the room looked terrible.
"I can fix the bookcase, Mr. Sleeby," said Mr. Mudanza, "but do you mind if I change it just a little?"
"All right," said Mr. Sleeby.
First Mr. Mudanza carried all the books upstairs to Mr. Sleeby's bedroom.

Can you picture that bookcase with no books?

Then he took out all the shelves.

Can you see the bookcase with no books and no shelves?

Next he took the bookcase out to Mr. Sleeby's backyard.

Can you picture a bookcase with no shelves and no books in a backyard?

Mr. Mudanza laid the bookcase on its back in the grass.

Can you picture a bookcase with no shelves, lying on its back in a yard?

Finally he filled the bookcase with sand.

Can you picture Mr. Sleeby's bookcase with no shelves, lying in a backyard and filled with sand?

130 **Mr. Mudanza Changes Things for Mr. Sleeby**

"You've changed my bookcase into a sandbox," said Mr. Sleeby. "Say, that's great! A lot of children play in my yard, and I had nothing for them to play with. A sandbox is just the thing!"

Mr. Sleeby looked around at all the things Mr. Mudanza had fixed for him.

"It's wonderful of you to fix so many things," said Mr. Sleeby. "I have a new door, a new bed, a new jacket, and a new sandbox. The only trouble is, it makes me see that the rest of my house is in bad shape."

"I could change your house a little, Mr. Sleeby," said Mr. Mudanza. "Would you mind?"

"No," said Mr. Sleeby. "Go ahead. You always seem to change everything into something I want."

First Mr. Mudanza took out all the wooden floors and stairs, so the house had just a cement floor.

Can you picture that house with no wooden floors or stairs?

Next he took out all the insides of the house, so there weren't any rooms in it any more.

Can you picture that house with no walls except the outside ones and no wooden floors or stairs?

Finally he cut a great big hole in one side from the ground up and put in a great big door that would slide up and down.

Can you picture that house with no inside walls or wooden floors and with a great big sliding door in one side?
Does it look like a house?
What does it look like? (a garage)

"Say," said Mr. Sleeby. "You've changed my house into a garage. Thanks a lot. I've never had a garage. Now I can buy a car."

"I'll bet you have the biggest garage in town," said Mr. Mudanza.

Mr. Sleeby looked pleased, but then suddenly his face fell.

"What's wrong?" asked Mr. Mudanza.

"I just realized that I don't have a house any more," said Mr. Sleeby. "What will I do without a house?"

"I can fix that," said Mr. Mudanza. "I notice you have a teacup here with a broken handle. Do you mind if I change it a little?"

"Not at all," said Mr. Sleeby. "Since I don't have a house, I don't need a teacup."

First Mr. Mudanza laid boards on the ground, spreading out from the teacup. He nailed them together right under the teacup.

Can you picture those boards going out from under the teacup?

Then he laid more boards over them and covered the whole thing with shingles, under the teacup.

Can you picture that teacup on top of the boards and shingles?

Then he put up some posts and raised the whole thing on the posts.

Can you see those boards and shingles on top of the posts, with the teacup on the top of the whole thing?

Finally he filled the spaces between the posts with bricks and put in doors and windows. He did a lot of work inside, too.

Can you see those brick walls with doors and windows and shingles on top and a little teacup way up at the top of the whole thing? Does it look like just a teacup any more? What does it look like? (a house)

"It's a house!" cried Mr. Sleeby. "Thanks a lot!"

"Not at all," said Mr. Mudanza. "It was *your* teacup."

"And I was thinking of throwing away that teacup," said Mr. Sleeby. "Am I ever glad I didn't!"

43
I Know All About Goldilocks

One night Mrs. Breezy was telling stories to Mark, Willy, Portia, Manolita, and Ferdie. "Here's a story I'll bet you don't know," said Mrs. Breezy. "It's about Goldilocks."

"Oh, we know all about Goldilocks," said the children.

"Yes, Mother," said Mark, "that's the story about three bears who lived in the woods. One day the bears went for a walk, and Goldilocks came into their house. She ate Baby Bear's porridge, she sat in Baby Bear's chair and broke it, and then she went to sleep in Baby Bear's bed. When the bears came home, Goldilocks woke up and was scared of them and ran away."

"I guess you do know about Goldilocks," said Mrs. Breezy.

"I know all about Goldilocks, too," said Ferdie. "Listen. It's about three bears who lived in the woods. One day the bears went for a walk, and Goldilocks came into their house. She sat in Baby Bear's chair and broke it to pieces, and then she went to sleep in Baby Bear's bed. When the bears came home, Goldilocks woke up and was scared of them and ran away."

Did Ferdie remember all the parts of the story?

"Wait a minute," said Portia, "you forgot about the porridge."

"Oh, yes," said Ferdie. "When Baby Bear came home he was hungry, so he ate his porridge."

Is Ferdie right about the porridge?
Why couldn't Ferdie be right about Baby Bear coming home and eating his porridge?

"No, Ferdie," said Portia, "Goldilocks ate Baby Bear's porridge."

"Well," said Ferdie, "I forgot only one thing. Besides, I don't see why Goldilocks would want to eat porridge. I don't even know what porridge is."

"It's something like oatmeal," said Mrs. Breezy.

"Oh," grumbled Ferdie, "if I'd known it was oatmeal, I'd have remembered it. I know all about oatmeal."

I Know All About Goldilocks 133

"I'm sure you do," Mrs. Breezy said, "but I'm afraid you don't quite know all about Goldilocks."

"I wish I knew all about Goldilocks," said Willy.

"I'll bet you know quite a bit," said Mrs. Breezy. "Why don't you tell us about it and we'll see."

"This is all I remember," said Willy. "Three bears lived in the woods and one day they went for a walk. Goldilocks came to their house and ate all of Baby Bear's porridge, and then she went to sleep in Baby Bear's bed. When the bears came back, Goldilocks was afraid of them and ran out of the house."

Did Willy remember all the parts of the story?

"That's pretty good," said Manolita, "but you forgot one part. You left out the part about Baby Bear's chair."

"Yes," said Ferdie. "Baby Bear came home and sat down in his chair."

Is Ferdie right about the chair?
Why couldn't Ferdie be right about Baby Bear coming home and sitting in his chair?

"No," said Willy, "I remember now. Goldilocks broke Baby Bear's chair. So Baby Bear couldn't sit in it when he came home."

"I believe I can remember all the parts," said Manolita, "if I use my magic."

"Go ahead," said Mrs. Breezy.

Manolita waved her wand over the book and said, "Story, story, come into my head." Then she began: "Once upon a time there were three bears who lived in the woods. They went for a walk. Goldilocks came into their house. She ate Baby Bear's porridge. She sat on Baby Bear's chair and broke it. She went to sleep in Baby Bear's bed. Then the bears came home and thought some magic had happened."

Did Manolita get every part of the story right?

"No, Manolita," said Portia. "You forgot the ending."

"That's right, Manolita," said Ferdie. "Goldilocks woke up and talked with the bears."

Is Ferdie right about the ending?
What really happened at the end?

"That's not what happened," said Manolita. "I remember now. Goldilocks woke up and was scared by the bears, and she ran away."

"Am I ever going to get a turn?" asked Portia.

"Yes," said Mrs. Breezy. "It's your turn right now."

"Good!" said Portia. "Well, three bears lived in the woods and they went for a walk. Then Goldilocks came to the house, and she gobbled up Baby Bear's porridge and she broke Baby Bear's chair, and when the bears came home, she was scared of them and she ran away."

Did Portia remember all the parts of the story?

"No, Portia," said Ferdie. "You left out the part about the bed. Goldilocks stood on Baby Bear's bed and looked out the window. She saw the bears coming home and she ran away before they got in the house."

Is Ferdie right about the bed?
What really happened?

"You're just making that up," said Portia. "I remember now what really happened. Goldilocks fell asleep on Baby Bear's bed, and she woke up when the bears came home."

"I think you all did very well," said Mrs. Breezy. "But, Mark, I wonder how you knew so much about Goldilocks. I don't remember ever telling you the story before."

"You didn't tell me the story, Mother," said Mark. "Mrs. Nosho told me the story about Goldilocks. And when Mrs. Nosho tells you a story, you have to find out most of it yourself. That's how I know all about Goldilocks."

Portia's Lost Shoe

Portia had a pair of shiny white shoes that she loved. One morning she woke up and found only one shoe by her bed. She looked all around the bedroom, but she couldn't find her other shoe. She became very upset.

"I'll bet I know where it is," said Ferdie. He looked in the closet. It wasn't there. "I give up," Ferdie said. "I can't think of anywhere else it could be."

Would you give up?
Can you think of any other places a shoe could be?

Just then Mark came over to play. "Why are you upset, Portia?" he asked.

"I lost one of my shiny white shoes!" Portia cried. "I was always afraid I'd do that. I even had my name and address written in them so they wouldn't get lost, and now one of them got lost anyway!"

"I lose things sometimes, too," said Mark. "When I do, I find it helps to ask questions."

"Then please ask some questions," said Portia, "if it will make my shoe come back."

"All right," said Mark. "When was the last time you wore your white shoes?"

"I wore them to a party yesterday."

"What did you do on the way home from the party?"

"I ran a race with Ferdie."

"Did anything happen while you were running the race?"

"Yes, I stepped in some mud."

"Why are you asking all these dumb questions?" said Ferdie.

Why do you think Mark is asking those questions?

"Did you step in the mud with both feet?" Mark asked.

"No, with just one foot. I got mud all over one shoe."

"Did you track mud on the stairs when you got home?"

"No, I didn't," said Portia. "If I did, I would have had to clean it up."

"Then I think we should look out in the hall," said Mark.

136　Portia's Lost Shoe

Why did Mark think they should look in the hall?

They ran into the hall and looked all over, upstairs and downstairs, but they didn't find the shoe.

"That was a bad guess," said Ferdie.

Do you think it was a bad guess that the shoe might be out in the hall?
Can a guess be wrong and still be a good guess?

Portia said, "I think it was a good guess, because I remember now that I did take off my muddy shoe before I went upstairs."

"I know," said Ferdie. "A dog took it—the dog that lives in the basement!"

They ran down to the basement and looked around. Mrs. Dodd, who owned the dog, helped them look around her apartment, too. Even the dog helped them look. But no shoe was found.

"You bad dog," said Ferdie, "what did you do with Portia's shoe?"

Could they be sure that Mrs. Dodd's dog had taken the shoe?
What else might have happened to the shoe?

"That was a good guess, that the dog took the shoe," said Mark. "But it might not be right. Let's try some more questions. Who comes in and goes out of your hallway? Start in the morning. Who's the first person who comes in or goes out?"

"The milkman," said Portia.

"I know!" said Ferdie. "The milkman took it! I'll bet he thought it was a milk bottle—because it is white."

Is that a good guess? Why not?
Does a shoe look much like a milk bottle?

"Who's the next person who comes in or goes out?" Mark asked.

"Mother," said Portia. "She goes to work."

"I know!" said Ferdie. "I'll bet Mother put on your shoe and wore it to work."

Is that a good guess?
Why not?

"*Then* who comes in or goes out?" Mark asked.

"Then Loretta the Letter Carrier comes in, to bring us letters and packages," said Portia.

"Loretta the Letter Carrier. H'm," said Mark. "She's always doing things to help people. Did you say that your shoe had your name and address in it?"

"Yes," Portia said.

"Then I think I know where to look."

Where do you think Mark will look?
Why might Loretta have put the shoe in the mailbox?

They looked in the mailbox, and, sure enough, there was Portia's white shoe. Inside the shoe was a note from Loretta the Letter Carrier. It said, "Dear Portia: I found this shoe on the front steps. Whoever mailed it to you forgot to put a stamp on it. But it had your name and address, so I put it in your box. Please tell your friends that, after this, when they send you a shoe, they should wrap it up, put a stamp on it, and drop it in a mailbox. Your friend, Loretta the Letter Carrier."

Portia's Lost Shoe

45

Mr. Sleeby Jumps

Mr. Sleeby heard that Willy had broken his leg and was in the hospital, so he went to the hospital to see him. Willy was lying in bed. His leg was held up in the air by a rope, and there was a big, heavy cast on his leg to keep it from bending.

"I see that you won't be doing much walking for a while, Willy," said Mr. Sleeby.

"That's right," said Willy. "I wish I could. I'll be happy when my leg is well, so I can jump and hop and stamp my foot again. Do you like to jump and hop and stamp your foot, Mr. Sleeby?"

"I think I do," said Mr. Sleeby, "but I'm not sure I remember what those words mean. What is jumping?"

"That's when you lift both feet off the floor, Mr. Sleeby," said Willy.

"Like this?" asked Mr. Sleeby. [Demonstrate lifting one foot after the other, as in marching.]

Was that jumping?
Why wasn't it jumping?

"No, Mr. Sleeby," said Willy. "When you jump, you lift both feet at the same time."

"Oh," said Mr. Sleeby, "like this." [Demonstrate a good jump.] "So that's jumping. Yes, I like to do that."

"Now what are those other things you asked me about?" said Mr. Sleeby.

"I asked if you like to hop," said Willy.

"Oh, yes. What's hopping?"

"Hopping," said Willy, "is when you keep one foot off the floor."

"Like this?" asked Mr. Sleeby. [Demonstrate lifting one foot and keeping it in the air.]

Was that hopping?
Why wasn't it hopping?

"No, Mr. Sleeby," said Willy. "When you hop, you keep one foot up like that, but then you jump with the other foot."

"Oh," said Mr. Sleeby, "like this." [Demonstrate a good hop.]

"What was that other thing?" asked Mr. Sleeby.

"I asked if you like to stamp," said Willy.

"Oh, yes. What's stamping?"

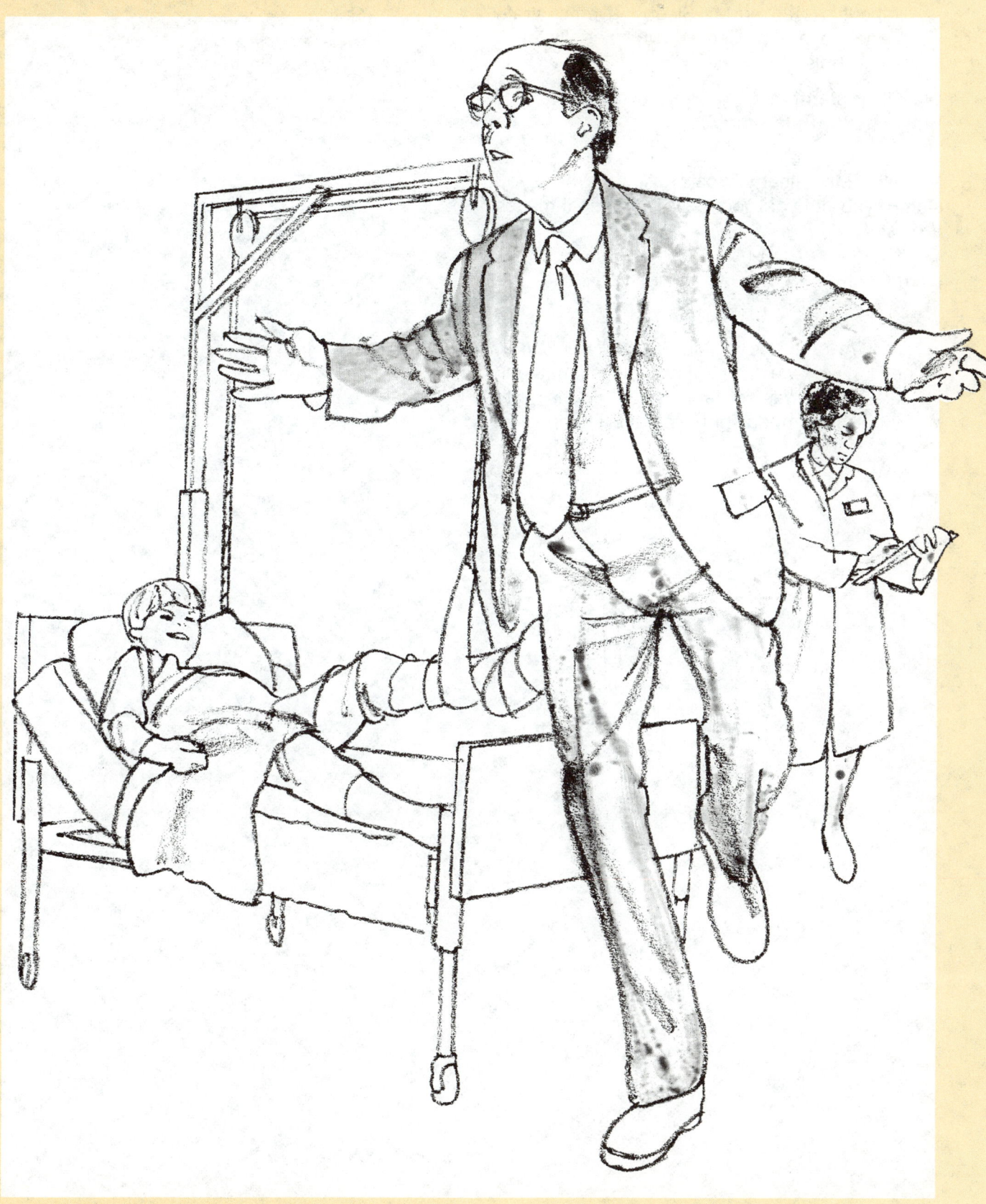

"Stamping," said Willy, "is when you lift one foot and put it down."

"Like this?" asked Mr. Sleeby. [Demonstrate lifting one foot and putting it down so gently that it makes no noise.]

Was that stamping?
Why wasn't it stamping?

"No, Mr. Sleeby," said Willy. "When you stamp, you put your foot down hard, so it makes a noise."

"Oh," said Mr. Sleeby, "like this." [Demonstrate a good stamp.]

"You're pretty good, Mr. Sleeby," said Willy. "When I'm well, we can do those things together."

Mr. Sleeby was so happy about his visit with Willy that he jumped, hopped, and stamped all the way home.

46

The Lion Who Roared like a Waterfall

Note: See story 27, "The Chicken Who Practiced to Be Queen," for suggestions on presenting this kind of story.

Mrs. Nosho was telling Mark a story about a lion.

"This lion," said Mrs. Nosho, "was king of all the jungle animals, but he thought he could be a mightier king if only he could do one thing better."

"Pardon me," said Mark. "I have a question."

What question do you think Mark will ask?

Mark asked, "What did the lion want to do better?"

"He wanted to roar louder," said Mrs. Nosho. "He already had a loud roar, but he wanted to roar even louder. So he asked the owl what he should do, and the owl told him to go take lessons from this thing that roared louder than a lion."

"Pardon me," said Mark. "I have another question."

What do you think Mark will ask?

Mark asked, "What was this thing that roared louder than a lion?"

"It was a waterfall," said Mrs. Nosho. "There was a great waterfall in the river, and when the water came rushing over the waterfall it made a roar that was louder than ten lions. Well, every day the lion practiced trying to roar just like the waterfall. After a few weeks the lion thought something that wasn't true."

"Pardon me," said Mark.

What question do you think Mark will ask?

Mark asked, "What did the lion think that wasn't true?"

Mrs. Nosho answered, "The lion thought that he was learning to roar louder, when actually his roar was getting quieter. The waterfall had fooled him, you see."

"Pardon me," said Mark.

What question do you think Mark will ask?

141

Mark asked, "How did the waterfall fool the lion?"

"It happened this way," said Mrs. Nosho. "The river was drying up, and every day less water came over the waterfall, so the waterfall was getting quieter and quieter.

"Soon it was only as loud as five lions, then only as loud as two lions, then the river dried up so much that the waterfall was only a trickle and it wasn't as loud as half a lion. And the lion kept trying to roar like the waterfall, so he was getting quieter too, but he didn't know it.

"Finally, when the lion had decided that he could roar just like a waterfall, he went back to his village and ordered all the jungle animals to gather around him. Then he opened his mouth to roar, and all the animals laughed at the sound that came out of his mouth."

"Pardon me," said Mark.

What do you think Mark will ask?

"What was the sound that came out of the lion's mouth?" Mark asked.

"The sound that came out of his mouth," Mrs. Nosho said, "wasn't a roar at all. It was 'Trickle, trickle, trickle.' The animals all laughed, and then the giraffe said something and they laughed some more."

"Pardon me," said Mark.

What do you think Mark will ask?

Mark asked, "What did the giraffe say?"

"The giraffe said, 'I thought we had a lion for a king, but he sounds more like a leaky faucet.' "

The Lion Who Roared like a Waterfall

How to Get Exactly What You Want

"Come along, Mark," said Mr. Breezy. "I'm going shopping, and if you come along, I'll teach you how to buy things."

Mark was happy to go along, because he liked to learn how to do things.

"Now the main thing to remember," said Mr. Breezy, "is always to tell the salesperson exactly what you want."

First they went to a used-car lot where there were all kinds of cars for sale.

"Listen carefully," said Mr. Breezy, "and hear how I tell the salesman exactly what I want."

When the salesman came up, Mr. Breezy said, "Good afternoon. I'd like to buy a very special kind of car. I'll tell you exactly what kind of car I want. I want a car with four wheels and windows and a motor and a steering wheel."

Did Mr. Breezy tell the salesman exactly what kind of car he wanted?
What's wrong with what Mr. Breezy told the salesman?

"I'm sorry," said the salesman, "but I'm not sure what kind of car you want. All our cars have four wheels and windows and a motor and a steering wheel. Could you tell me more about what kind of car you want?"

"All right," said Mr. Breezy, "I'll tell you more. I want a car with headlights and doors and a top. I want a car that when you stick a key in it and turn the key, it starts going."

Will the salesman now know what kind of car Mr. Breezy wants?
Why not?

The salesman shook his head. He still didn't know what kind of car Mr. Breezy wanted, because all his cars had headlights and doors and a top and they all started with a key. So the salesman pointed to a big blue car and asked, "How would you like this one?"

"I'm afraid this car won't do," said Mr. Breezy. "It's too big and it has only two doors and it's not red."

"Oh," said the salesman, "now I think I know what kind of car you want."

How to Get Exactly What You Want 145

What kind of car do you think Mr. Breezy wants?
Why do you think so?

The salesman showed Mr. Breezy a little red car with four doors. "That's exactly what I want," said Mr. Breezy. "I'll take it."

As they drove away in the little red car, Mr. Breezy said to Mark, "You see, if you *tell* the salesperson exactly what you want, you'll *get* exactly what you want."

Next they went to a clothing store. Mr. Breezy said to the salesclerk, "Good afternoon. I know exactly what I want, so this won't take long. Let's see, I want something that's made of cloth and that's something to wear, and it should be sewed together with thread."

Did Mr. Breezy tell the salesclerk exactly what he wanted?
What's wrong with what Mr. Breezy told the salesclerk?

"I'm sorry," said the salesclerk, "but I'm still not sure what you want. Almost everything in our store is made of cloth and is something to wear and is sewn together with thread. Could you tell me more about what you want?"

"All right," said Mr. Breezy, "I'll tell you more. I want something that looks nice and that covers part of me and that I can take off when I'm through wearing it."

Will the salesclerk now know what Mr. Breezy wants?
Why not?

The salesclerk brought Mr. Breezy a blue shirt.

"That's not quite right," said Mr. Breezy. "You see, it's not brown and the cloth is too thin, and it won't fit over my legs, and there's no way to hold it up with a belt."

"Oh," said the salesclerk, "now I think I know what you want."

What do you think Mr. Breezy wants?
Why do you think so?

The salesclerk brought Mr. Breezy a pair of pants made of thick brown cloth and with loops for a belt. "That's exactly what I want," said Mr. Breezy. "I'll take them."

Then they went to a pet shop to buy Mark a pet.

"Do you think you could tell a salesclerk exactly what you want?" Mr. Breezy asked Mark.

Do you think *you* could tell a salesclerk exactly what you want?
Would you do it the way Mr. Breezy does? Why not?

"I don't know if I can remember everything," said Mark. "Sometimes I have trouble remembering things. But I'll try."

When the saleswoman in the pet shop came up to them, Mark said, "Good afternoon. I know exactly what I want, so this won't take long—or at least I hope it won't. I want . . . I want a baby white rabbit."

"I think we have just what you want," said the saleswoman, and she went to the back room to look for it.

Mr. Breezy looked unhappy. He told Mark, "You tried, son, but you forgot some things. You forgot to say that the rabbit should have four legs and a fluffy tail. You forgot to say that it should have a nose and two eyes and long ears and soft fur. If you want to get exactly what you want, you have to say all those things."

Should Mark have said all those things?
Would they help him get the kind of rabbit he wanted? Why not?

In a minute the saleswoman came back with a little white rabbit. Mark was surprised. "This is exactly what I want!" he said.

"You were lucky that time," said Mr. Breezy. "It's not easy to tell people exactly what you want. But you're learning. Before long you'll be able to ask for things the way I do."

Was Mark just lucky? Why did he get what he wanted?
Who did the better job of saying exactly what he wanted, Mark or Mr. Breezy?

I Know All About Mr. Sleeby

"Do you know Mr. Sleeby?" asked Portia.

"Yes, I do," said Loretta the Letter Carrier. "We're very good friends. I know all about Mr. Sleeby."

"I know that Mr. Sleeby forgets things," said Portia, "and I know that he's nice to children, but that's all I know about him."

Do you know anything else about Mr. Sleeby? What do you know?

"I'll tell you some more about Mr. Sleeby," said Loretta. "Mr. Sleeby is very, very thin and he doesn't have much hair on top of his head. In the winter you would think that his head would get cold, but he never wears a hat. He likes to eat in restaurants, and he always dresses up in his best and newest clothes when he goes to eat in a restaurant. I know Mr. Sleeby very well. That's how I know all these things about him. Can you remember all these things, Portia?"

"I can remember most of them," said Portia. "I remember that he's thin and that he never wears a hat. I remember that he likes to eat in restaurants and that he always dresses up when he does."

What did Portia forget?

"You forgot that he doesn't have much hair on top of his head," said Loretta.

"Oh, yes," said Portia.

"I know all about Mr. Sleeby, too," said Ferdie. "I know that he has just been to the barber and had a haircut because his hair was coming down over his eyes."

**Does that sound right to you?
Why couldn't what Ferdie said be true?** (Mr. Sleeby hasn't much hair on top of his head.)

Then Ferdie said, "I know that Mr. Sleeby went to eat in a restaurant because he loves to eat in restaurants."

**Does that sound right to you?
Did Ferdie say anything that couldn't be true that time?** (no)

"But before he went to the restaurant," said Ferdie, "he went home and put on his old work clothes."

What's wrong?
What did Ferdie forget about Mr. Sleeby? (Mr. Sleeby always wears his best clothes to a restaurant.)

Ferdie also said, "Mr. Sleeby had a little trouble getting through the restaurant door because he's so fat."

Does that sound right to you?
What did Ferdie forget about Mr. Sleeby? (Mr. Sleeby is very thin.)

"When he got inside the restaurant," said Ferdie, "he hung up his hat and sat down to eat."

Does that sound right to you?
Now what has Ferdie forgotten about Mr. Sleeby? (Mr. Sleeby never wears a hat.)

"I think you forgot some things," said Loretta. "You forgot that Mr. Sleeby is thin and doesn't have much hair and never wears a hat, and you forgot that he always dresses up when he eats in a restaurant."

"But you remembered that he likes to eat in restaurants," said Portia. "That was good remembering, Ferdie."

"I'll tell you some more about Mr. Sleeby," said Loretta. "He always wakes up early in the morning, even though he doesn't have an alarm clock. And all he watches on TV is the news. He eats his breakfast in a restaurant because he loves to eat out and, besides, he can't cook. Then he rides to work on the bus because he likes bus rides. Can you remember all these things, Portia?"

"I think so," said Portia. "I remember that he wakes up early and that he doesn't have an alarm clock. I remember that all he watches on TV is the news and that he rides to work on the bus."

What did Portia forget?

"You forgot that he eats breakfast in a restaurant and that he can't cook," said Loretta.

"Oh, yes," said Portia.

"I know more than that about Mr. Sleeby," said Ferdie. "I know he's late to work sometimes because he forgets to wind his alarm clock."

Does that sound right to you?
What did Ferdie forget? (Mr. Sleeby has no alarm clock and always wakes up early.)

"I know something else," said Ferdie. "Mr. Sleeby baked himself some cookies and had some milk with them for breakfast."

What's wrong?
What has Ferdie forgotten about Mr. Sleeby this time? (Mr. Sleeby can't cook and he eats breakfast in a restaurant.)

Ferdie said, "After Mr. Sleeby ate breakfast, he watched a movie on TV."

Does that sound right to you?
What did Ferdie forget? (Mr. Sleeby watches only news on TV.)

Then Ferdie said, "When Mr. Sleeby goes to work, he drives pretty fast."

What's wrong?
What did Ferdie forget about Mr. Sleeby? (Mr. Sleeby rides to work on the bus.)

Portia asked Ferdie, "How do you know so much about Mr. Sleeby?"

"I just know," said Ferdie, "because I'm smart."

Do you think Ferdie knows a lot about Mr. Sleeby?
What do *you* know about Mr. Sleeby?
Can you think of any things you *don't* know about Mr. Sleeby?

"I wish I knew more about Mr. Sleeby," said Portia. "I don't know if he likes dandelions. I don't know if he can roller-skate. I don't know if he steps on ants."

"That's funny," said Loretta. "I don't know those things either. I guess I don't know all about Mr. Sleeby after all."

The Pig in the Tree

Note: See story 27, "The Chicken Who Practiced to Be Queen," for suggestions on presenting this kind of story.

Mrs. Nosho was telling Mark a story about a pig.

"Once upon a time," said Mrs. Nosho, "there was a pig who was too proud to work and too proud to talk to the other animals. All he did was lie around and sleep. That's why some girls were able to play such a trick on him."

"Pardon me," said Mark. "I have a question."

What question do you think Mark will ask?

Mark asked, "What trick did the girls play on the pig?"

Mrs. Nosho answered, "While the pig was asleep, the girls picked him up and put him high in the top of a tree. When the pig woke up, he was frightened and didn't know how to get down from the tree—because a pig, of course, can't climb. So the pig started to do something."

"Pardon me," said Mark. "I have another question."

What do you think Mark will ask?

Mark asked, "What did the pig do?"

"The pig started to cry for help," said Mrs. Nosho. "'Oink! Oink!' he cried, 'Someone come help me!' In a little while something came to help him, but the pig said 'I'm too proud to do that. It would scratch my lovely belly.'"

"Pardon me," said Mark.

What do you think Mark will ask?

"What came to help the pig?" Mark asked. "What was it going to do?"

"An eagle came to help the pig. It was going to carry him down in its claws.

"The pig went on crying for help, and soon something else came to help him, but the pig said, 'I'm too proud to do that. It would make blue spots on my pretty pink skin.'"

"Pardon me," said Mark.

150

What do you think Mark will ask?

Mark asked, "What came to help the pig? How would the pig get blue spots on his skin?"

"Someone who had been picking blueberries came to help him," said Mrs. Nosho. "That person offered to let him jump down into a basket of soft blueberries.

"Then something else came to help him, but the pig said, 'I'm too proud to do that. It would make me look foolish.' "

"Pardon me," said Mark.

What do you think Mark will ask?

Mark asked, "Who came to help him? What would make the pig look foolish?"

"A giraffe came to help him," said Mrs. Nosho. "It offered to let the pig slide down its long neck. Then the giraffe said something that made the pig think a little, so that finally the pig did slide down the giraffe's neck. And that's how the pig got out of the tree."

"Pardon me," said Mark.

What do you think Mark will ask?

Mark asked, "What did the giraffe say that made the pig think?"

Mrs. Nosho answered, "The giraffe said, 'If you're afraid of looking foolish, you'd better grow feathers and sing like a bird, because a pig in a tree is in danger of looking foolish no matter what he does.' "

Index of Stories

Chicken Who Practiced to Be Queen, The 81
Coffee at Grandmother's House 97
Farmer Who Found a Giant in His Barn, The 91
Ferdie and the Big Boys 84
Ferdie and the Pot 12
First Things First 59
House Where Sleeby Dwells, The 27
How Mr. Sleeby's House Got That Way 31
How to Get Exactly What You Want 144
I Forgot What You Needed 43
I Know All About Goldilocks 132
I Know All About Mr. Sleeby 147
It's Hard Work to Be a Boss 56
Lion Who Roared like a Waterfall, The 141
Loretta Delivers the Valentines 106
Manolita Loves Magic 50
Manolita's Answer Machine 78
Manolita's Real Magic 62
Manolita's Second Magic Machine 87
Mark at the Bath 71
Mark the Builder 122
Mark Wraps a Present 40
Mr. Mudanza 46
Mr. Mudanza Buys Christmas Presents 74
Mr. Mudanza Changes Things for Mr. Sleeby 128
Mr. Sleeby Buys New Furniture 116
Mr. Sleeby Jumps 138
Mr. Sleeby Tells About the Circus 68
Mr. Sleeby Thinks He's a Giant 2
Mr. Sleeby's Toy Store 100
Mrs. Nosho Gets Ready for a Trip 65
Mrs. Nosho in Her Yard 53
New Neighbors, The 119
Pig in the Tree, The 150
Poor Old Bowser 18
Portia's Birthday 38
Portia's Lost Shoe 135
Shovel in the Basement, The 35
Something Green for Mrs. Nosho 9
Thing That Went Under the Door, The 7
Three Bowsers, The 103
Two of Everything 94
What's Your Trouble, Mr. Sleeby? 110
Willy and Mrs. Nosho 15
Willy Keeps On Wishing 113
Willy the Wisher 4
Willy's Lost Kitten 125
Woman with the Wood, The 20
Would You Rather Have the Dog? 23